Chambers

perfect punctuation

Chambers

CHAMBERS
An imprint of Chambers Harrap Publishers Ltd
7 Hopetoun Crescent
Edinburgh EH7 4AY

This (second) edition published by Chambers Harrap Publishers Ltd 2005
Previous edition published as *Chambers Guide to Punctuation* 1999
© Chambers Harrap Publishers Ltd 2005

Reprinted 2006, 2008

A CIP catalogue record for this book is available from the British Library.

ISBN-13: 978 0550 10139 6

Designed and typeset by Chambers Harrap Publishers Ltd, Edinburgh
Printed and bound in Spain by Graphy Cems

CONTRIBUTORS

Editors
Ian Brookes
Kay Cullen

Series Editor
Elaine O'Donoghue

Publishing Manager
Patrick White

Prepress Manager
Sharon McTeir

Prepress Controller
Claire Williamson

CONTENTS

What is punctuation?

Punctuation is the system of non-alphabetical symbols that we use in writing to group words together, and to separate words and groups of words from each other. There are four main occasions when punctuation is used:

- to indicate the boundaries between sentences
- to indicate the boundaries between different areas within a sentence
- to separate words or groups of words from their surroundings
- to separate individual words (or sometimes letters) when they are combined to create a single unit of meaning

Why is punctuation important?

The importance of punctuation should be apparent if you try to read the following paragraph:

> its Anne Peter Ive come to take you home she said gently he made no outward sign that he had heard or understood her he was sitting hunched up in the corner hugging his knees which were drawn up to his chest eyes tightly closed and making a sound like an animal in pain he went on rocking himself slowly backwards and forwards backwards and forwards

Here is the same paragraph with punctuation included. Note, for example, how the presence of punctuation marks makes it clear to the reader which words are spoken and which are not, and that the words *in pain* should be taken with *like an animal* rather than with *he went on*:

> 'It's Anne, Peter! I've come to take you home,' she said
> gently. He made no outward sign that he had heard or
> understood her. He was sitting hunched up in the cor-
> ner, hugging his knees (which were drawn up to his
> chest), eyes tightly closed, and making a sound like an
> animal in pain. He went on rocking himself slowly
> backwards and forwards, backwards and forwards …

Clearly, punctuation makes writing and printing easier to read. It is an aid to comprehension on two levels: it gives the reader informa- tion about how the text might be read aloud using appropriate pauses and intonation; and, more importantly, it shows which words are to be taken together, and which are to be separated from each other, that is, how words relate to each other.

Using this book

This book is arranged in three parts:

- Part One deals with all the major punctuation marks in turn so that readers who want to explore the subject fully can famili- arize themselves with the rules and conventions that apply to each, and build on their knowledge as they move from one chap- ter to the next. This structure makes the book easy to dip into if information about the proper use of a particular punctuation mark – such as the comma, the semicolon, or the colon – is needed.

- Part Two deals with matters that concern punctuation in gen- eral, including situations when it may not be clear what sort of punctuation is required, special uses of punctuation, and the changing use of punctuation marks.

- Part Three looks at other devices that are used in writing to make life easier for readers. Such devices are especially important in the modern world where word-processing packages allow writers to use bold and italic type to do some of the work that has traditionally been done by punctuation.

Throughout the book, there are examples that illustrate clearly how a particular punctuation mark should or should not be used. The symbol ✔ before an example is the indicator of correct use, and the symbol ✗ identifies examples where punctuation has been used incorrectly.

Although this book attempts to provide useful rules for punctuating your writing, there are many variations that are acceptable. For example, you can sometimes choose to use or to omit a punctuation mark in a particular context without affecting the sense. However, it is important to remember that when there is such a choice, the method you adopt should be consistent throughout a piece of writing.

We hope that you will find that reading and using this book will give you a firm grasp of the concepts behind the use of punctuation, and that, as a result, your writing becomes clearer and more accurate.

Other Desktop Guides are: *Common Errors*, *Effective Grammar*, and *Letter Writing*. The *Chambers Good Writing Guide* provides useful tips on a wide variety of relevant topics including style, sensitive language and proofreading your own work.

Glossary

adjective a word that provides more information about a noun

adverb a word that gives information about when, how, where, why or in what circumstances something happens or is done

clause a sequence of words that includes a verb

compound noun a noun that consists of two or more words, such as *make-up* or *three-line whip*

compound verb a verb that consists of two or more words, such as *hang-glide* or *stir-fry*

conjunction a word that links words, groups or clauses, such as *and*, *but*, *because*

interjection a word class consisting of words and short phrases conveying some sort of emotion, such as *Ouch!* or *Wow!*

lower-case not in capitals, eg in the word *London*, the letters *ondon* are lower-case

main clause a clause that can stand on its own, eg *As soon as she arrived home, <u>she put on the kettle</u>*.

noun a word used to name people, places, things, ideas, etc, such as *Joe Bloggs*, *Paris*, *table*, *romance*, *bravery*

object the element in the clause that is involved in or affected by the action of the verb, eg in *he kissed <u>her</u>*, *her* is the object

phrasal verb a phrase, consisting of a verb and another short word, that functions as a verb, such as *blow over* or *set about*

plural indicating the presence of more than one examples of the thing being talked about, eg *cats* is the plural form of *cat*

prefix a group of letters does not form a word in its own right, but which can added to the beginning of another word to modify its meaning, such *anti-* or *un-*

pronoun a word such as *me* or *they* that can be substituted for a noun

proper name a name given to a particular person, place or thing, typically starting with a capital letter

relative clause a clause that is usually introduced by a relative pronoun, which identifies or gives more information about someone or something, eg *the girl <u>who is standing by the window</u> is my sister*

relative pronoun a pronoun such as *who* or *that*, which is used to introduce a relative clause

sentence a sequence of words, or sometimes a single word, which begins with a capital letter and ends with a full stop, question mark or exclamation mark

sentence fragment a group of words that begins with a capital letter and ends with a full stop, but does not convey any information by itself

singular indicating the presence of only one example of the thing being talked about, eg *cat* is a singular form, but *cats* is a plural form

subject the element in a clause which indicates the person or thing that is responsible for an action or process. It determines the form of a verb. In *he kissed her*, *he* is the subject

subordinate clause a clause that cannot stand on its own, but depends on a main clause or another subordinate clause to make sense, eg <u>*As soon as she arrived home*</u>, *she put on the kettle.*

upper-case in capitals, eg in the word *London*, *L* is an upper-case letter

verb a word that expresses actions, communication, mental processes and states of being, such as *be*, *run*, *think*, *sing*

Part One

The Punctuation Marks

The full stop

The full stop as a sentence marker

The main use of the full stop is to mark where sentences end. Most people are aware of the rule that a sentence should start with a capital letter and, when it is not a question or an exclamation, should end with a full stop. Thus, the full stop is the correct punctuation mark to use at the end of sentences that express complete statements, as in the following examples:

> *Our flight is due to leave at 6 o'clock.*
>
> *The new edition of Angling Times is available in the shops now.*

In a continuous block of text, there should be no space between the full stop and the last letter of each sentence. Note the use of full stops in the following passage:

> Jack Kerouac was born in Massachusetts in 1922. His childhood was happy, but various disasters upset the family, including the death of an older brother. Kerouac accepted a football scholarship at Columbia University, spent the early years of World War II working as a mechanic, then returned to his home town as a sports journalist. In 1942 he went to Washington, DC, where he worked briefly on the construction of the Pentagon before joining the US merchant marines, subsequently enlisting in the US navy in 1943. After only a month he was discharged and branded an 'indifferent character'.

His friends included Allen Ginsberg, Gary Snyder and Neal Cassady, whom Kerouac portrayed as Dean Moriarty in his most famous novel, *On the Road* (1957). Kerouac was identified as leader and spokesman of the 'Beat Generation', a label he coined then came to regret and repudiate. *On the Road* follows two friends as they weave their way across the USA. It is loose, apparently structureless and episodic, and it made Kerouac a cult hero. In later books, such as *The Dharma Bums* (1958) and *Big Sur* (1962), he flirted with Zen Buddhism. Kerouac died in 1969.

In many sentences, a full stop is the only punctuation mark necessary. This may even be the case in relatively long sentences, provided the parts of the sentence are closely connected to each other in sense or theme and are joined by a linking word, such as *and* or *because*, or a linking phrase, such as *so that* or *in order to*, as in the following examples:

She got up early and went for a long walk.

I usually go to the supermarket on Saturdays because it is the only day of the week I have free.

She makes soup from the chicken bones so that nothing is wasted.

He did a second job in the evenings in order to earn some extra money.

Sentences and sentence fragments

When you use full stops to punctuate a passage, make sure that you don't separate information that should belong in a single sentence into two sentences. A full stop should not be used if it would leave a 'sentence fragment': that is, a group of words that cannot stand on its own and make sense, as in the following examples:

✗ *There were no clues. As to what had happened.*

✗ *He has a large collection of old cartoons. Of which Tom and Jerry is his favourite.*

In both these examples, the second group of words carries no meaning by itself. There is in fact only one statement being made so the full stop should be removed or replaced by a comma, as follows:

✔ *There were no clues as to what had happened.*

✔ *He has a large collection of old cartoons, of which Tom and Jerry is his favourite.*

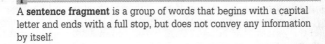

A **sentence fragment** is a group of words that begins with a capital letter and ends with a full stop, but does not convey any information by itself.

In normal speech, we often do not use complete sentences, and sentence fragments are very common. In informal writing, which tends to be influenced more by the customs of common speech than the strict rules of grammar, it can be legitimate to punctuate so as to leave sentence fragments, especially if they are very closely linked to the previous statement, as in:

✔ *I don't hate her. Far from it.*

✔ *At that moment a bowl of fruit fell on Tom's head. Unlucky for Tom.*

✔ *Will Tom ever catch Jerry? No chance.*

Remember that sentence fragments should not be used in formal writing, such as business correspondence or reports. Their use should be confined to informal correspondence, journalism or creative writing. However, even in informal contexts they should be used fairly sparingly unless you want to create a particular stylistic effect.

Position of the full stop when quoting direct speech

When punctuating direct speech that comes at the end of a sentence and ends with a full stop, the full stop comes *inside* the closing quotation mark. It is not necessary to add a second full stop outside the closing quotation mark:

> ✔ *He said regretfully, 'We seem to be out of cheese.'*

> ✗ *He said regretfully, 'We seem to be out of cheese.'.*

Note that when the quoted speech comes before the verbs of saying, wondering, etc, the full stop at the end of the quoted speech is replaced by a comma:

> ✔ *'We seem to be out of cheese,' he said regretfully.*

> ✗ *'We seem to be out of cheese.' he said regretfully.*

When the text in quotation marks comes at the end of a sentence, but what is inside the quotation marks is not direct speech, the full stop usually comes *outside* the closing quotation marks, as in:

> *At the bottom of each white cross were the words 'An unnamed soldier who fell in the Great War of 1914–18'.*

Omission marks

You will sometimes see not one but three full stops at the end of a sentence. This set of three full stops is known as 'omission marks' or 'suspension marks', and is used to indicate that a sentence or statement has gradually tailed off into silence, or that something further is implied but is not actually stated.

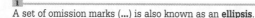

i

A set of omission marks (...) is also known as an **ellipsis**.

Consider the following examples:

> *Nothing she tried seemed to do any good. She was at her*

wits' end. The baby cried and cried...

And so, dear reader, let us avert our eyes and leave these two young lovebirds to their billing and cooing...

'This gun's loaded. If you don't give me the money...'

The first example uses omission marks to show how the crying of the baby went on continuously and relentlessly. In the second example, the writer is indicating to the reader that the couple's ongoing happiness is taken for granted and need not be described further. In the third example, the threat is left unfinished because what has already been said strongly implies that the person being threatened will be shot unless the money is handed over.

From the point of view of punctuation, note that, in all these examples, the sentence ends with only the three dots of the omission marks. Because their purpose is precisely to indicate that the sentence is unfinished, it is not appropriate to add a full stop to make a fourth dot. However, any new sentence after the three omission marks starts with a capital letter in the normal way.

If you are using a computer, you can create a set of omission marks (provided the 'Num Lock' feature is turned on) by holding down the 'Alt' key and typing 0133.

The full stop used to indicate abbreviations

Another use of the full stop is after a letter or group of letters to show that it is an abbreviated form of a longer word:

Dr. McLaren [= Doctor McLaren]

65 m.p.h. [= 65 miles per hour]

See fig. 3 [= See figure 3]

However, it is now common to write many abbreviations without a full stop. (For full information on abbreviations, see pages 125–30.)

The full stop in e-mail and website addresses

The full stop is also found in e-mail and website addresses as a marker to divide up the different elements of the domain name. In this use the full stop is usually referred to as a dot:

> *clementine@marketing.goldmine.com*
>
> *tomcat@mousetrap.co.uk*
>
> *Visit our website at www.chambers.co.uk.*

Checklist

1. **The full stop as a sentence marker**
   - used at the end of sentences that express complete statements

2. **Sentences and sentence fragments**
   - do not use a full stop if it will leave a group of words which does not make sense on its own
   - in informal writing, it is possible to leave occasional sentence fragments

3. **Position of the full stop when quoting direct speech**
   - when a quoted sentence comes at the end of a sentence, the full stop comes *inside* the closing quotation mark
   - when a quoted sentence comes before the verb of saying, it ends with a comma rather than a full stop
   - when something other than direct speech is inside the quotation marks, the closing full stop comes *outside* the closing quotation mark

4. **Omission marks**
   - used at the end of some sentences to indicate that something further is implied but not actually stated

5. **The full stop used to indicate abbreviations**
- to indicate that a letter or group of letters is an abbreviated form

6. **The full stop in e-mail and website addresses**
- to mark the break between parts of a domain name

Punctuation in practice

A Insert full stops in the correct places in these sentences:

1 *Tom was planning a surprise party for Jerry*

2 *Cindy stayed at home and tried on her new shoes*

3 *Add the butter and the condensed milk*

4 *My e-mail address, jane@easynet co uk, is easy to remember*

B Try inserting full stops and capital letters to make sense of the following short passage:

beside herself with rage and humiliation, she paced the floor grinding her teeth she was so focussed on thoughts of revenge that she didn't hear the door opening it wasn't until her mother was standing in her line of vision that she became aware that someone was actually witnessing her inarticulate mutterings and oaths she stopped in her tracks, suddenly more embarrassed than angry

The question mark

i

The **question mark** (?) is also known as an **interrogation mark**.

The question mark as an alternative sentence marker

We saw in the previous chapter that the end of a sentence is usually marked by a full stop. The question mark is one of two possible substitutes for the full stop at the end of a sentence. (The other is the exclamation mark, which is discussed in the next chapter.)

The use of a question mark at the end of a sentence indicates that what is written should be read as a question, and this will usually be obvious to the reader:

> *Where has that mouse gone to?*
>
> *Do you have any cheese?*

However, in some cases the appearance of a question mark at the end of a sentence may be the only indication to a reader that the sentence is a question rather than a statement, and thus should be read with the appropriate expression and tone. Compare the following examples:

> *You've had your lunch.*
>
> *You've had your lunch?*

The first example is a statement of fact and so is punctuated with a full stop. The second example is composed of the same words in the same order, but the writer is attempting to establish whether the statement is true, and this enquiry is signalled by the question mark at the end of the sentence.

Direct questions and indirect questions

As far as punctuation is concerned, there is an important distinction between direct questions and indirect questions.

Direct questions

A direct question occurs when the entire sentence constitutes an enquiry. The question mark is used at the end of direct questions, as in:

> *Do you realize who you're talking to?*
>
> *Would anyone like some brandy?*
>
> *What does he intend to do with that big pile of bricks?*

Indirect questions

An indirect question occurs when an enquiry is mentioned within a sentence but the words are not repeated in the exact form used by the questioner. Indirect questions are often introduced by *if* or *whether*. A question mark is not required at the end of a sentence that contains an indirect question. If the entire sentence is actually a statement or a command, rather than a question, use a full stop, as in:

> *She asked me if I realized who I was talking to.*
>
> *He asked whether anyone would like some brandy.*
>
> *You're probably wondering what he intends to do with that big pile of bricks.*

Be careful about long sentences that can appear at first sight to be questions, but are in fact statements, as in the following example:

✗ *But the really interesting question is what will take its place in this vital prime time slot?*

✔ *But the really interesting question is what will take its place in this vital prime time slot.*

When an indirect question is contained within a direct question, it is correct to use a question mark:

> *Did you ask your teacher if bringing pets to school was allowed?*
>
> *Why don't you enquire whether there is any cheese left over?*

A question mark is also used when what appears to be a statement containing an indirect question is, in reality, expressing a tentative request, as in:

> *I was wondering if you'd like to join us for dinner this evening?*
>
> *Perhaps you could ask your sister if you can borrow her car?*

Using a question mark to express uncertainty

The question mark does not always come at the end of a sentence. It can also be used inside brackets to draw attention to something that is questionable or uncertain in a text or statement, as in:

> *He said that his name was Tarquin Vanderwal (?) and he came from New York.*
>
> *St Patrick [389–?493], patron saint of Ireland, was born in Britain, probably somewhere in Wales.*

In the first example, the question mark draws attention to the fact that the author is not certain that the name has been recorded accurately; in the second, it shows that the date of St Patrick's death is not known for certain.

---

i

In 1962, Martin K Speckter invented a punctuation mark **?** called an **interrobang**. It was designed for use at the end of an exclamatory rhetorical question, eg 'You're going out wearing that?' Deriving its name from a combination of *interro*gation and 'bang' (printers' slang for an exclamation mark), the interrobang does not seem to have caught on.

Checklist

1. **The question mark as an alternative sentence marker**
   - for sentences that express questions rather than statements

2. **Direct questions and indirect questions**
   - direct questions require a question mark
   - indirect questions do not require a question mark

3. **Using a question mark to express uncertainty**
   - a question mark can be placed inside brackets to express uncertainty

Punctuation in practice

A Which of these sentences should end with a question mark, and which with a full stop?

   1 *Did I ask you about your trip to Italy*

   2 *Whether she will come now is anybody's guess*

   3 *The question that immediately comes to mind on reading the report is why this problem was not identified earlier*

   4 *I don't suppose you would give some thought as to how we can improve the situation*

B Try inserting capital letters, full stops and question marks to make sense of the following short passage:

was it only four hours since her sisters had gone to the party she asked herself whether they would come back soon and tell her all about it in the meantime there was not much point sitting around and dreaming the housework would not do itself, would it cindy looked around for the duster where on earth had she left it

The **exclamation mark** (!) is also known (especially in American usage) as an **exclamation point**.

The exclamation mark as an alternative sentence marker

It was mentioned in the previous chapter that the exclamation mark is one of two possible substitutes for a full stop at the end of a sentence. As with the question mark, an exclamation mark may be the only indication to the reader of the way that the sentence should be read: that is, whether the writer's words should be read as a matter-of-fact statement, a question, or an exclamation. Compare the following sentences, which differ only in terms of punctuation:

> *You've tidied your room.*
>
> *You've tidied your room?*
>
> *You've tidied your room!*

In the first sentence, the full stop indicates that the speaker is simply reporting a fact; in the second, the question mark shows that the speaker is asking whether a statement is true; in the third, the exclamation mark shows that the speaker is expressing surprise at a fact.

There are five types of sentence that may require an exclamation mark:

THE EXCLAMATION MARK

Interjections

Interjections are words or phrases that stand on their own as sentence fragments (see pages 4–5) and express strong emotion. They are followed by an exclamation mark:

> *There, there!*
>
> *Doh!*
>
> *Tut, tut!*
>
> *Aargh!*

Expressions of strong emotion

An exclamation mark can be used to indicate a tone of surprise, or some other strong emotion such as admiration, anger, frustration or desperation. Here are some more examples:

> *How you've grown!*
>
> *What a beautiful picture!*
>
> *Don't you dare swear at me, you little twerp!*
>
> *I don't believe it!*
>
> *Help me! I'm falling!*

Emphatic statements

The exclamation mark is also used in certain other expressions that are emphatic statements of the speaker's opinion, such as:

> *Oh no, not that old chestnut again!*
>
> *What a fool I've been!*
>
> *You are an absolute life-saver!*

Exclamatory questions

An exclamation mark is the correct punctuation mark to use for what are known as exclamatory questions: that is, sentences that have the form of a question but are, in fact, exclamations.

Here are some examples:

> *What the blazes are you doing!*
>
> *Isn't this great!*
>
> *Wasn't that a marvellous surprise!*

Commands

Sentences that express an order or command may or may not end with an exclamation mark. A mild command can be punctuated with a full stop, but a more emphatic command should be punctuated with an exclamation mark, as in the following sequence:

> *'Sit down, all of you.'*
>
> *No one moved.*
>
> *'Sit down when I tell you!' he shouted.*

The use of exclamation marks in formal and informal writing

In all sorts of writing, exclamation marks are used to reflect the tone and expression when recording spoken language. When not recording spoken language, there is a distinction to be made between the use of exclamation marks in formal and informal writing.

In informal writing, such as in a personal letter, exclamation marks are often used to emphasize a particular remark, as in:

> *It was a real tonic to see you all last weekend!*
>
> *Your kindness and hospitality was much appreciated!*

The exclamation mark is also used in this sort of writing to show that what has just been said is a jokey comment or aside, as in:

> *He's quite amazing for someone of his age. He'll want to take up skydiving next!*

THE EXCLAMATION MARK

However, where a more formal style of writing is expected, as in reports and business correspondence, exclamation marks should generally be avoided:

✗ *We recommend that you proceed with extreme caution!*

✔ *We recommend that you proceed with extreme caution.*

---

i

Excessive use of exclamation marks to indicate emphasis or humour has been widely discouraged and condemned. F Scott Fitzgerald once said disapprovingly that using an exclamation mark was like laughing at your own joke.

Checklist

1. **The exclamation mark as an alternative sentence marker**
   - after interjections
   - after expressions of strong emotion
   - after emphatic statements
   - after exclamatory questions, in preference to a question mark
   - after commands, depending on the degree of emphasis

2. **The use of exclamation marks in formal and informal writing**
   - in informal writing, exclamation marks are more widely used to indicate the mood and feelings of the writer
   - in formal writing, exclamation marks are usually used only when reporting speech

Punctuation in practice

A Which punctuation mark should be used to mark the end of these sentences?

1 *What a glorious sunset*

2 *Stop making that horrible noise immediately*

3 *The committee is extremely enthusiastic about your proposal*

4 *Wasn't that a fantastic save by the goalkeeper*

B Try inserting capital letters, full stops, question marks and exclamation marks to make sense of the following short passage:

'i don't believe it we leave you alone for one day and you turn the house into a disaster area there isn't a scrap of food anywhere what on earth have you been doing' her stepmother stormed off into the other room five seconds later she screamed out, 'good grief somebody is asleep in my bed'

The apostrophe

The use of the apostrophe to show omission

The apostrophe is used in shortened forms of words to indicate
where letters or numbers have been omitted, as in *I've* for *I have*,
can't for *cannot*, *the '50s* for *the 1950s*, and *the '68 Olympics* for *the
1968 Olympics*.

It also appears in poetic short forms, such as *'twas* for *it was* and
e'er for *ever*, and in some hyphenated words that contain a shortened word, such as *will-o'-the-wisp* for *will of the wisp* and *ne'er-
do-well* for *never do well*.

Sometimes it may not be obvious that the apostrophe indicates
omission because the longer form is not often heard. For example,
o'clock is a short form of *of the clock* and *fo'c'sle* is a short form of
forecastle.

However, there are some shortened forms that are now commonly
spelt without an apostrophe. The apostrophe was formerly used in
words such as *'bus* (for *omnibus*), *'plane* (for *aeroplane*), *'flu* (for
influenza) and *'cello* (for *violincello*). Nowadays it would be regarded
as old-fashioned to use an apostrophe in these 'clipped' forms,
although you may still see an apostrophe used in older texts.

Note that *won't* and *shan't* are written with only one apostrophe, even though letters are omitted in two places. However, where *and* is shortened to *'n'* there are two apostrophes, as in *rock'n'roll* and *salt'n'vinegar* crisps.

> **Usage**
>
> Abbreviations such as *don't* and *shouldn't*, that are created by running two words together, have the apostrophe at the place where letters are omitted, rather than the place where the first word ends.

The use of the apostrophe to show possession

The second main use of the apostrophe is to form 'possessives' – word-forms that indicate ownership or possession. When an apostrophe is used to indicate possession it is generally followed by an *s*. There are four situations to consider:

For singular nouns and names that end with a letter other than *s*, the possessive is formed by adding *'s*, as in the following examples:

> *Holly's hair is getting darker as she gets older.*
>
> *The child's hands were cut and bleeding.*
>
> *This coat is Mary's, I think.*

Note that when possession applies to two or more named individuals, the *'s* is added to the last name only, as in:

> *Do you have John and Adele's address?*
>
> *All of Tom and Jerry's friends came to the party.*

For plural nouns that end with a letter other than *s*, the possessive is also formed by adding *'s*, as in the following examples:

> *The children's education is more important than anything else.*

the people's love of ceremony

the men's hostel

For singular nouns and names that end in *s*, the possessive form is usually formed by adding *'s*, as in:

These are James's CDs.

a photograph of Agnes's mother and father

my boss's car

the bus's rear bumper

the octopus's normal food

However, note that an apostrophe without a following *s* is used to form the possessive of names ending in *-es*, where the word is made up of more than one syllable. This is also the convention in certain other names, including names from the Bible and the ancient world:

That is John Hodges' house.

Ulysses' wife

Moses' parting of the Red Sea

Keats' poems

Jesus' mother, Mary

Xerxes' army

For plural nouns and names that end in *s*, the possessive is formed by adding an apostrophe only, as in:

the ladies' room

the Joneses' garden

two dollars' worth [= the amount two dollars will buy]

three months' holiday [= a holiday of three months]

the octopuses' tank

Usage

The basic rule for singular and plural nouns that end in *s* is: **write what you hear and say**. If an extra *s* is added in the spoken pronunciation of the possessive form, then add *'s* in the written form. However, if it sounds too clumsy to add a second *s*, add an apostrophe only.

Occasionally, a form that was originally a possessive loses its apostrophe as it becomes thought of as a word in its own right, rather than the possessive form of another word. Therefore, there is no apostrophe in *gents*, although this means a *gentlemen's lavatory*. Similarly, it is no longer necessary to have an apostrophe in the expression *for goodness sake*, even though, strictly speaking, the noun *goodness* is used as a possessive [= for the sake of goodness]. Thus, *for goodness's sake* is now never used, and *for goodness' sake* is becoming rare.

Warning: apostrophes and pronouns

Apostrophes are often used incorrectly in possessive forms of pronouns. Pronouns are short words such as *it*, *her* and *they*, that can be used as substitutes for a noun. The possessives of these words are not formed according to a regular pattern, and if a pronoun happens to have an associated possessive form that ends in *s*, an apostrophe is not used. Here are some examples:

> *Are all these shoes hers?*
>
> *The neighbours' car is much bigger than theirs.*
>
> *I don't rate their new logo. Ours is much better.*
>
> *Yours sincerely*

Remember, in particular, that *it's* with an apostrophe is **not** the possessive form, but is rather the short form of *it is*. Note that the apostrophe in the shortened form *it's* comes before, not after, the *s*:

  ✗ *The team has lost it's last five matches.*

  ✔ *The team has lost its last five matches.*

  ✗ *Its' nearly 10 o'clock.*

  ✗ *Its nearly 10 o'clock.*

  ✔ *It's nearly 10 o'clock.*

Remember, also, that the possessive form of *who* is *whose*; *who's* with an apostrophe is the shortened form of *who is*. Compare the following examples:

  ✗ *Who's coat is this?*

  ✔ *Whose coat is this?*

  ✗ *Whose that at the door?*

  ✔ *Who's that at the door?*

Note, however, that an apostrophe is used in the possessive forms *someone's*, *anyone's* and *one's*, as in:

> *A trip in such a small aircraft is unlikely to cure one's fear of flying.*

> *It's anyone's guess.*

Warning: apostrophes and plurals

Even if you remember nothing else about punctuation, there is one point that you should make an effort to fix in your mind. Getting it wrong may cause people to dismiss anything you write as illiterate nonsense. This is it: as a general rule, **never** add an apostrophe in front of the *s* you use to form a plural, as in:

  ✗ *AUBERGINE'S 50p*

  ✗ *CREAM TEA'S*

  ✗ *The boy's walked down the street.*

The first two examples contain the so-called 'greengrocer's apostrophe', often seen in shop signs, price lists and advertising boards. All these examples are wrong, not least because a reader could be forgiven for asking, 'How did an aubergine get 50p and is it investing it wisely?' or 'The boy's *what* walked down the street?'

Exceptions

An apostrophe is allowed to form a plural in some exceptional cases, such as the plurals of certain short words, individual letters, numbers, and abbreviations made up of lower-case letters. For these plurals, the chance that the reader may hesitate or mispronounce what is written is avoided by the addition of the apostrophe. Here are some examples:

> *It's one of those posh do's.*
>
> *All the houses have lean-to's at the back.*
>
> *Mind your p's and q's.*
>
> *How many t's are there in your surname?*
>
> *Many football clubs have become plc's.*
>
> *The judges awarded them five 5.6's and four 5.7's.*

Another instance when it is permissible to add an apostrophe when forming a plural is when the plural is the title of a book or play, as in:

> *There have been two Macbeth's* [= two different versions of the play *Macbeth*] *staged in Tokyo this summer.*

THE APOSTROPHE

Punctuation in practice

A Here are some sentences with words that have apostrophes missing. Take care to add an apostrophe only to those words that should have one:

1. *Its time we put the budgie back in its cage.*

2. *Theyll get back home at about one oclock in the morning our time.*

3   *I couldnt brake quickly enough and now my sons bike has a buckled front wheel.*

4   *Its all curled up into a ball so you cant see its head.*

5   *Isnt this anyones newspaper? If it isnt, Ill take it home with me.*

6   *Ive been reading Keats poems.*

7   *Youll have to decide which is yours and which is hers.*

8   *Ones financial situation is surely ones own business?*

B Try making the following phrases possessive using an apostrophe or an apostrophe + *s*:

Example: *the house of my father*   *my father's house*

1   *the workshop of the blacksmith*   ....

2   *the children of the Smiths*   ....

3   *the toys of the children*   ....

4   *the masts of the boats*   ....

5   *the surgery of Dr Charles*   ....

6   *the rear wheel of the Mercedes*   ....

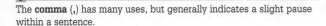

The comma

The **comma** (,) has many uses, but generally indicates a slight pause within a sentence.

The comma in lists

When a sentence contains a list of items of broadly equal importance, commas may be used to separate the different items. Here are some straightforward examples:

> *She grows potatoes, carrots, beans and onions.*

> *Alice, Siobhan and Liam will be coming to the party too.*

Note that the commas can be seen as substitutes for linking words; they are used to avoid repeating the word *and* after each item in the list. Without commas, you would have to write:

> *She grows potatoes and carrots and beans and onions.*

> *Alice and Siobhan and Liam will be coming to the party too.*

The items on the list do not have to be single words; they may also be phrases made up of several words:

> *Many of them find work in gift shops, fast-food joints and transport services.*

> *The wooden cooking utensils, hand-carved sticks and Loden capes in the Alpine shops are good value for money.*

Lists of adjectives

When a list is made up of a series of adjectives describing a noun, commas are usually added in the same way as described above:

It is a quiet, comfortable hotel close to the sea.

In his outstretched hand was an unremarkable, small and misshapen lump of what appeared to be dirty glass.

Where only two adjectives precede the noun, and these adjectives are not linked by *and*, the comma can sometimes be omitted. Note, however, that the presence or absence of a comma in a list of adjectives can be significant for making the meaning clear. Consider the following example:

A short, bearded butler showed them into the study.

With the comma, it is clear that the butler is short and also has a beard. But now look at the same sentence with the comma omitted:

A short bearded butler showed them into the study.

Is it the butler or his beard that is short? The possibility of confusion means that the comma is useful for clarifying the meaning.

In other sentences, however, there is no possibility of confusion if the comma is omitted:

The endangered white rhino is now being successfully bred in captivity.

The difference between this sentence and the previous example is that the adjectives *endangered* and *white* do not refer equally to the same word. Grammatically speaking, *white* modifies the noun *rhino*, but *endangered* modifies the phrase *white rhino*. Thus *endangered* and *white* are not part of a list.

THE COMMA

Here are some more examples of sentences with lists of adjectives that should not be separated by commas:

> *Just inside the gate was a great big dog.*

> *She wore a pair of antique Spanish earrings made of solid gold.*

Usage

A useful test to help you decide whether or not there should be a comma between two adjectives is to substitute an *and* for the comma. If the sense is clear with the *and* instead of the comma, this indicates that the adjectives are working as a list and so a comma is needed between the adjectives.

The serial comma

When you are writing a list of items, it is conventional to use a linking word such as *and* or *or* between the **last two** items even if you use commas between the other items in the list. Because you already have a linking word, it is not necessary to insert a comma between the last two items. However, a comma in this position is not incorrect, and some people prefer it, as in:

> *She grows potatoes, carrots, beans, and onions.*

> *Alice, Siobhan, and Liam will be coming to the party too.*

> *Do you want to go to the theatre, the museum, or an art gallery?*

This comma between the last two items in a list is known as a 'serial comma' or 'list comma'. Whether or not to include a serial comma is a matter of choice, although – as with other optional aspects of punctuation – you should be consistent in your choice.

In more complex lists, it is often advisable to insert a serial comma in order to avoid ambiguity:

> *The series will include material from some of Britain's most popular and innovative comedians: Tommy Cooper, Morecambe and Wise, Tony Hancock, and Vic Reeves and Bob Mortimer.*

If there were no comma after *Hancock*, the uninformed reader might be misled into thinking that Tony Hancock and Vic Reeves worked together as a double act.

The use of commas to mark off extra information within a sentence

Another use of commas is to mark off information that is to be treated as separate from or supplementary to the rest of the sentence.

A pair of commas can enclose extra information in much the same way as a pair of brackets. The words within the commas are effectively isolated from the rest of the sentence so that they do not interrupt the flow or sense. In this way, the words surrounded by the commas are rather like a verbal 'aside', which you hear but which doesn't divert you from the main topic of conversation. Here are some sentences in which commas are used in this way:

> *He maintained that he, as the only surviving male, had a legitimate claim to the throne.*
>
> *It was her opinion, she told Rory, that there was something awfully funny going on.*
>
> *A second earthquake, less severe than the first, caused minor damage.*
>
> *Janine, like her mother before her, is a very competent horsewoman.*
>
> *She had, of course, no other choice.*
>
> *Carol, who hated being the centre of attention, was extremely embarrassed.*

THE COMMA

In all these sentences the supplementary comment is surrounded by **a pair of commas**. If you forget the second comma, you will probably be left with an incomplete sentence:

✔ *Malcolm, who you already know, is related to me by marriage and is a regular houseguest.*

✘ *Malcolm, who you already know is related to me by marriage and is a regular houseguest.*

Note, also, that the commas should be positioned so that if the words they enclose were to be removed, the sentence would still make sense. Look at the following example:

✔ *He got to his feet and, clearing his throat loudly a couple of times, began to speak.*

✘ *He got to his feet, and clearing his throat loudly a couple of times, began to speak.*

A useful check is to look at the sentence with the supplementary phrase removed. If the sentence still makes sense without it, the commas are positioned correctly. We can apply this test to the examples above:

✔ *Malcolm [...] is related to me by marriage and is a regular houseguest.*

✘ *Malcolm [...].*

✔ *He got to his feet and [...] began to speak.*

✘ *He got to his feet [...] began to speak.*

Usage

You can use this procedure as a handy test to check whether you have positioned the commas correctly in a sentence.

Commas and relative clauses

> **i**
>
> A relative clause is a group of words within a sentence that gives extra information about the person or thing just mentioned. A relative clause begins with a 'relative pronoun', such as **who**, **which** or **that**.

Relative clauses are a special case of additional information being inserted into the sentence. You can often recognize these clauses because they begin with a 'relative pronoun', such as *who*, *which* or *that*. For example, the italicized words in the following examples indicate relative clauses:

> *Carol, who hated being the centre of attention, was extremely embarrassed.*
>
> *The thing that annoys me most is that he doesn't seem to care.*
>
> *The workers, who have already accepted a pay cut, have protested about the proposed merger.*
>
> *Her new book, which was published last year, has received rave reviews.*
>
> *The house that I'm looking for has a long driveway.*

When punctuation is being considered, it is important to know that there are two distinct types of relative clause:

- A **non-defining relative clause** makes a comment or gives additional information about the noun it refers to. This type of relative clause is separated off from the rest of the sentence by being enclosed in a pair of commas.

- A **defining relative clause** serves to identify or pick out the noun it refers to. This type of relative clause is not enclosed by commas.

33

Consider one of the previous examples again:

> *The workers, who have already accepted a pay cut, have protested about the proposed merger.*

Here, the presence of the commas indicates that *who have already accepted a pay cut* is a non-defining relative clause. It does not restrict the application of the word *workers* to those who have accepted a pay cut. All of the workers have accepted a pay cut and all have protested.

However, removing the commas changes the meaning:

> *The workers who have already accepted a pay cut have protested about the proposed merger.*

Now, *who have already accepted a pay cut* is a defining relative clause, and its effect is to restrict the application of the word *workers* to only those people who have accepted a pay cut. They are the ones who have protested.

Do you mean all of the workers or just some of them? Take care to punctuate the sentence according to the sense you want to convey.

Sentence adverbs

A 'sentence adverb' is a word or phrase that comments on or gives extra information about the whole sentence. When such a word or phrase is inserted into a sentence as a comment, it should be marked off from the surrounding sentence by a pair of commas:

> *Soon after Michaelmas, however, Bruce descended with a large force into England.*
>
> *It was, I'm afraid, just the sort of low-down trick I've come to expect from them.*

Sentence adverbs that come at the beginning or end of a sentence are marked off from the rest of the sentence by a single comma:

> *Nevertheless, she can't be expected to do it all immediately.*
>
> *However, this isn't what we're here to talk about today.*
>
> *Economically, the news was an absolute disaster.*
>
> *You'll have to retype the whole thing, I'm afraid.*

Words such as *yes*, *no* or *please* should be marked off with commas when they are part of a longer sentence:

> *Two ice-cream cones, please.*
>
> *No, I think you're wrong about that.*

Names of people being addressed by the speaker

The name of a person or group of people being addressed by the speaker should also be marked off by commas. Here are some examples:

> *You, Jim, are the person Harry has to liaise with over this.*
>
> *Now, ladies and gentlemen, would you please start moving through to the dining room.*
>
> *Mary, do you know where my hairbrush is?*

The use of the comma to mark off clauses

Commas can be used to mark off the different parts, or 'clauses', that make up a long sentence.

Sentences with two main clauses

Many sentences consist of two parts of equal weight, joined by a linking word such as *and* or *or*, as in this example:

> *John giggled, but Henry turned deathly pale.*

THE COMMA

The two parts or 'main clauses' have equal weight in this sentence. One clause contrasts with the other, and both clauses could, if necessary, stand alone as complete sentences:

> *John giggled. Henry turned deathly pale.*

In sentences where two main clauses are linked, the first clause should be followed by a comma. Here are some more examples:

> *Gary was a very promising artist, yet he couldn't get a place in art college.*
>
> *Great minds think alike, and fools seldom differ.*
>
> *The Yukon is ideal for those of you who enjoy roughing it in the wilderness, but British Columbia is a less challenging holiday destination for the average tourist.*

Note, however, that if the same person or thing is the subject of two linked clauses, a comma is not required:

> *John ran into the shop and asked for a copy of Angling Times.*
>
> *On Thursdays we usually go to the cinema or look around the shops.*

Sentences with a subordinate clause before the main clause

Another type of sentence consists of two unequal parts: a main clause that describes an action and a 'subordinate clause' that qualifies the action, for example by saying when, where, how or why it happened.

When a subordinate clause beginning with a word such as *when*, *how*, *since*, or *although* is placed at the beginning of a sentence, before the main clause, a comma must be inserted after the last word in the subordinate clause. Here are some examples that illustrate this use of the comma:

> *When he arrived home, the children ran to hug him.*
>
> *As soon as she heard the news, she booked a seat on the first flight home.*
>
> *Since a majority of people has voted in favour, planning permission for the proposed development is hereby granted.*
>
> *Soon after their daughter was born, they visited Ashok's grandparents.*
>
> *Although he was still weak, he managed to walk around the garden.*

Sentences with a main clause followed by a 'result' clause

When a sentence consists of a main clause followed by a subordinate clause, whether or not a comma is required between the clauses depends on the type of information in the subordinate clause.

When the subordinate clause expresses a result or consequence of the action referred to in the main clause, the subordinate clause should usually be separated from the main clause by a comma, as in:

> *She works night shifts, so her mother looks after the children during the day.*
>
> *All the lights went out, so we had to eat by candlelight.*

Note that if a comma is omitted, the following clause expresses 'purpose' rather than 'result':

> *She is working overtime so she can save up for holiday.*
>
> *The lights were dimmed so it would seem more romantic.*

There is an exception to the rule that a comma should be added before a result clause. When a result clause is linked to the main clause by the linking word *and*, no comma is necessary:

> *Write on the walls of your bedroom again and there'll be no TV for a month.*

The use of the comma to clarify meaning

Sometimes it is necessary to clarify the structure or meaning of a written sentence by inserting a visual break. The comma serves this purpose and can be used to prevent the reader from being misled by taking together two words that stand next to each other but do not belong together grammatically. Look at these sentences and note how the presence or absence of a comma, or its position, changes the sense:

> *He was sick, and tired of trying to make a living in a place that was so obviously dying on its feet.*
>
> *He was sick and tired of trying to make a living in a place that was so obviously dying on its feet.*
>
> *For one week only, coats will be half-price.*
>
> *For one week, only coats will be half-price.*
>
> *Outside the square was a seething mass of angry demonstrators.*
>
> *Outside, the square was a seething mass of angry demonstrators.*

Take care, however, not to insert a clarifying comma that has the effect of separating the subject from the verb, as in:

✗ *The dress that she wore to the party, is the one she bought in Paris.*

✔ *The dress that she wore to the party is the one she bought in Paris.*

When two identical words appear together, a comma may be inserted between them to avoid confusion:

✔ *What sort of husband he is, is of no interest to his employer.*

✔ *If she can, can you let me know.*

The use of the comma in dates

If the date is written in the order 'day/month/year', no comma is required between the month and the year, as in:

> *30th August 1998*
>
> *30 August 1998*

However, if the order is 'month/day/year', a comma must be inserted between the day and the year, as in:

> *August 30, 1998*

If the day of the week is named, a comma should be inserted between the name and number of the day, as in:

> *Sunday, 30 August 1998*

Three places where commas should not be used

While it is obviously very important to know where a comma should be inserted, it is almost as important to know when not to use one.

Do not use a comma to link what are, in fact, two separate sentences:

✘ *The caterpillars of the cabbage white butterfly will destroy your brassicas in a matter of days, rabbits will do the same.*

THE COMMA

✔ *The caterpillars of the cabbage white butterfly will destroy your brassicas in a matter of days. Rabbits will do the same.*

Do not use a comma when the second part of the sentence explains the purpose of or the cause behind the first, indicated by a linking word such as *and*, *because* or *that*:

✘ *He was tired, because he had stayed up until 3 o'clock.*

✔ *He was tired because he had stayed up until 3 o'clock.*

✘ *Penny told you yesterday, that she might be a little late for work this morning.*

✔ *Penny told you yesterday that she might be a little late for work this morning.*

We have already noted that adverbs that comment on the entire sentence, rather than a single word or phrase, should be marked off from the surrounding sentence by a pair of commas. However, do not insert commas to mark off adverbs – or phrases that act as adverbs – unless you intend them to be read as a commentary on the entire sentence. Consider the following pairs of examples:

The British research and development establishments were, curiously, reluctant to employ them.

The British research and development establishments were curiously reluctant to employ them.

Of course, she was lying.

Of course she was lying.

Both pairs of examples are punctuated correctly. However, in the first pair the use of commas changes the function of the adverb: *curiously* applies to the whole sentence in the first sentence, and only to *reluctant* in the second. In the second pair, the omission of the comma changes the phrase *of course* from a comment to a confirmation. Take care to punctuate a sentence according to how you want it to be read.

Checklist

1. The comma in lists
- to mark off the items in a list instead of using *and*
- a comma is not required in a string of adjectives if you could not substitute the word *and* for it
- some people prefer to insert a 'serial comma' between the last two items in a list, even if the word *and* is present

2. The use of commas to mark off extra information within a sentence
- commas should be placed so that the information marked off by them can be deleted and still leave a complete sentence
- commas should be used to mark off 'non-defining' relative clauses but not 'defining' relative clauses
- commas should be used to mark off sentence adverbs
- commas should be used to mark off the names of people being addressed by the speaker

3. The use of the comma to mark off clauses
- to separate two main clauses of equal weight
- to mark the end of a subordinate clause that precedes the main clause of a sentence
- to separate the main clause of a sentence from a following subordinate clause that expresses a result or consequence

4. The use of the comma to clarify meaning
- placed between two words to prevent the reader from misreading the text

5. The use of the comma in dates
- between the day and the year when the date is written in the form 'month/day/year'
- between the day of the week and the number of the day when the day is named

> **6. Three places where commas should not be used**
> - to link two separate sentences
> - when the second part of the sentence explains the purpose of or the cause behind the first
> - around an adverb that you do not intend to apply to the entire sentence

Punctuation in practice

A Here are some sentences that have no commas between the capital letter at the beginning and the full stop at the end. Where should commas be placed to punctuate the sentences correctly?

1 *It was the longest most boring journey I've ever had to endure.*

2 *He had a big lump on his head a fractured wrist a bruise on his cheek and a small cut above his right eye.*

3 *The driver braked violently and flinging open the car door jumped out and grabbed the boy by the collar.*

4 *Even in 1950 however beer production was largely regional if not local and there were still some 310 firms with 540 separate breweries.*

5 *As the train pulled into the station heads popped out of every window.*

6 *Hey Harry have you got a moment?*

7 *Clumsily like a fallen horse righting itself she scrambled to her feet gathered up the bananas marshmallows umbrella thermos handbag and other possessions that had fallen or rolled around her and waving reassuringly walked briskly away.*

B Try inserting capital letters and punctuation marks to make sense of the following short passage:

> tom who had been standing around idly in the street saw his friend approaching jerry was carrying a large bag which was stuffed full of eggs cheese tomatoes and mushrooms 'hey jerry where have you been' 'i was feeling hungry so i decided to go to the shops and get some food so I could make a big tasty omelette'

The colon

i

The **colon** (:) generally promises that what comes next will elucidate what has just been said.

The use of the colon to introduce a clarification

The principal use of the colon in ordinary texts is to indicate that what follows explains, expands on, or completes the part that has gone before. What follows the colon may be a complete sentence, a list, or even a single word. Here are some examples of sentences punctuated by colons:

I've got some really exciting news: Kirsty got the job in London.

It is certainly the best book I have read on the subject: well-researched, amusing, and packed with fascinating information.

He has one of those pompous-sounding titles: Executive in Charge of Stationery Fastenings, or something of that kind.

We made mountains of sandwiches: cheese and pickle, ham, roast beef, and lettuce and tomato.

Four of United's players are injured and will miss the big game: James, Stanton, Garcia and Volkov.

All the time she was at the health farm she thought of one thing, and one thing only: food.

However, you should avoid inserting a colon after the verb *to be*:

> ✗ *In these situations, by far the most important thing is:*
> *keep calm.*

> ✔ *In these situations, by far the most important thing is to*
> *keep calm.*

Lists

The colon is the correct punctuation mark to use when introducing a 'tabulated' list, in which each item stands on a new line:

> *For wallpapering, you should have the following equipment:*
>
> > *a pasting table*
> >
> > *a pasting brush*
> >
> > *a paper-hanging brush*
> >
> > *a broom*
> >
> > *a clean bucket with a handle*
> >
> > *a wallpaper trough*
> >
> > *wallpaper scissors*

The use of the colon to introduce direct speech

A colon may be used, in strictly limited ways, to introduce direct speech or quoted material from another piece of writing. These uses of the colon are dealt with in detail on pages 98 and 100.

Other uses of the colon

It is also worth noting a few specialized uses of the colon.

Ratios

Colons are used between numbers to indicate ratios:

49:28 = 7:4

a 4:1 vote in favour

In formal writing, however, it is preferable to write out ratios in full:

The devastating range of the longbow and the skill of the archers won the battle for the English, though they were outnumbered by the French by nearly three to one.

After headings in memos

Colons are used after headings in memos and certain other types of business writing:

To: Cinderella

From: Prince Charming

Cc: Ugly Sisters

Re: Slippers

Before subtitles

A colon is also used in the titles of books, reports or other publications where there is a main title followed by a subtitle or subsidiary title:

The declining population of domestic mice: a statistical survey

1. **The use of the colon to introduce a clarification**
- to indicate that what follows explains, expands on, or completes the part that has gone before
- to introduce a list

2. **The use of the colon to introduce direct speech**
- see pages 98 and 100

3. **Other uses of the colon**
- in ratios
- after headings in memos
- before subtitles

Punctuation in practice

Where should a colon be inserted in these sentences, and where is a comma also needed?

1 *Here is the fruit you asked me to get a pound of grapes four oranges and half a dozen bananas.*

2 *The Life of Oscar Wilde Tragedy or Farce?*

3 *I'm sure I've packed everything suntan lotion swimwear mosquito repellent film for the camera passports and money.*

4 *This is exactly what I wanted a room with a view over the harbour.*

The semicolon

---

i

The **semicolon** (;) is stronger than a comma but not as strong as a full stop.

The use of the semicolon to mark a break between clauses

We saw in a previous chapter that two 'main clauses' can be combined using a comma and a linking word to form a single sentence. It is also possible to use a semicolon to join two main clauses to make a longer sentence. Bear in mind the following points if you are tempted to use a semicolon to join two main clauses:

- A semicolon can be used only where the two clauses may otherwise stand as two complete sentences: whenever a semicolon is used, there is also, in principle, the option of using a full stop instead. The decision to use a semicolon is based on stylistic choice rather than grammatical necessity.
- The use of a semicolon makes the relationship between the two clauses closer than two separate sentences would, but creates a stronger break than is provided by a comma and a linking word.
- If a semicolon is used, there is generally no linking word.
- The semicolon has the effect of balancing or contrasting what is said in one clause and what is said in the following clause.

Here are some examples of sentences where semicolons mark the break between clauses:

A crocodile is a reptile; a whale is a mammal.

There's no more to be said; the matter is closed.

Children at play are not playing about; their games should be seen as their most serious-minded activity.

Traditionally many legal documents have been written without punctuation; in modern documents punctuation is more common.

Note that, in all these examples, the clauses separated by the semicolon could stand as separate sentences. Moreover, the semicolon could also be replaced by a comma and a linking word or 'conjunction'.

Do not use a semicolon when the second part of the sentence is not capable of standing as a sentence in its own right. Consider the following examples:

✗ *I wasn't worried; even when the other team scored.*

✗ *She had achieved that rarest of sporting achievements; a hole in one.*

In each case, the last part of the sentence is not capable of making sense on its own. Therefore, neither example should be punctuated by a semicolon. In fact, the first should have a comma and the second a colon:

✔ *I wasn't worried, even when the other team scored.*

✔ *She had achieved that rarest of sporting achievements: a hole in one.*

In general, when the clauses are connected by a linking word, the punctuation mark to use between the clauses is a comma rather than a semicolon. However, certain connecting words that have the function of explaining how an argument is progressing are preceded by a semicolon. These include *however*, *hence*, *thus*, *therefore*, *meanwhile*, *also*, *consequently* and *nevertheless*.

THE SEMICOLON

Here are some examples of sentences that have one of these connecting words preceded by a semicolon:

> *She was standing right in front of him; however, he couldn't see her.*

> *There were frantic attempts to save personal belongings; meanwhile, the water level continued to rise.*

> *The goods were not delivered on the date specified; therefore, we have cancelled the order.*

The use of the semicolon to mark off items in lists

As we saw on page 28, the comma is usually the correct punctuation mark to use to separate the items in lists. However, in some long sentences, using commas may not make clear where the division falls between items. This might happen, for example, because some of the items on the list are grammatically quite complex and contain commas themselves. In such cases, using semicolons can help to identify where the breaks come in a complex list, thus allowing the reader to pause at a logical point in the sentence. The following examples illustrate this use of the semicolon:

> *There was an alpine garden of saxifrages, sempervivum and sedum; a herbaceous border of hostas, aquilegias and delphiniums; and at the far end a wall of fuchsia and rhododendrons.*

> *There have been several recent studies on the subject: from Germany there is The End of the History of Art; from Britain, a group of essays entitled The New Art History; from the United States, Rethinking Art History; and from Canada there is the bluntly titled Art History: its use and abuse.*

> **Checklist**
>
> 1. **The use of the semicolon to mark a break between clauses**
> - to mark a stronger and more definite break in a sentence than a comma, but less of a break than that between two separate sentences
>
> 2. **The use of the semicolon to mark off items in lists**
> - in complex lists where using commas to mark off the items would lead to confusion

Punctuation in practice

Here are some sentences in which it might be appropriate to use a semicolon. There are missing commas and full stops in these sentences too. Where can a semicolon be used, and where should other punctuation marks go?

1 *Dickens is my favourite author Trollope is a close second*

2 *You shouldn't regard this as a setback see it instead as a pause for reflection*

3 *The country's wealth was built on the more traditional industries of steel-making shipbuilding and heavy engineering textiles clothing and carpet manufacture pottery and glassmaking and coal-mining*

4 *Both France and Italy have had to take steps to reduce government spending consequently the unemployment rate in both countries has risen significantly*

Quotation marks

Quotation marks (' ... ', " ... ") work in pairs to surround actual speech and quotations, or to highlight certain words or phrases. Quotation marks are also known as **quotes** or **inverted commas**.

The use of quotation marks to enclose speech and quotations

Quotation marks are used to mark off 'direct speech' and 'direct quotations': that is, the exact words someone has spoken or written. Here are some examples:

> *'Why can't I go?' asked Charlotte.*
>
> *They chanted in unison, 'We want more!'*
>
> *'To the true cynic', said Oscar Wilde, 'nothing is ever revealed.'*

Note that, in the last example two sets of quotation marks are needed, because the quotation has been split into two parts. It is important to remember that quotation marks enclose only **the exact words** used by the speaker, and not a reported version of these words.

The act of mentioning what has been said without repeating the exact words of the speaker is called 'indirect speech' or 'reported speech', and in these cases quotation marks are **not** used. The following sentences are examples of indirect speech:

> *Charlotte asked her mother why she could not go.*
>
> *They all chanted that they wanted some more.*

Oscar Wilde said that nothing is ever revealed to the true cynic.

When speech is not reported in the exact words of the speaker, quotation marks are not required. Compare the following sentences:

✔ *He nudged her and whispered, 'Do you want to leave now?'* [= direct speech]

✔ *He nudged her and asked in a whisper if she wanted to leave now.* [= indirect speech]

✘ *He nudged her and asked in a whisper 'if she wanted to leave now'.* [= indirect speech]

Similarly, if a quotation is reworded so that it does not reproduce the original exactly, the quotation marks should be moved so that they only surround what remain of the exact words, or they should be dropped altogether. The following examples reproduce F Scott Fitzgerald's exact words:

F Scott Fitzgerald said, 'An exclamation mark is like laughing at your own joke.'

'An exclamation mark,' to quote F Scott Fitzgerald, 'is like laughing at your own joke.'

Both are direct quotations and are therefore enclosed by quotation marks.

If the words are expressed indirectly or their order is changed, they should not be enclosed in quotation marks:

✔ *F Scott Fitzgerald said that an exclamation mark is like laughing at your own joke.*

✘ *F Scott Fitzgerald said that 'an exclamation mark is like laughing at your own joke'.*

However, it is possible to use quotation marks around a short phrase that is preserved intact when a quotation is expressed indirectly:

> ✔ *F Scott Fitzgerald said that an exclamation mark is 'like laughing at your own joke'.*

The positioning of other punctuation marks in sentences that contain quotation marks is worth looking at in detail, and is discussed fully on pages 96–102.

The use of quotation marks to highlight words in a sentence

Quotation marks are sometimes used by writers to highlight or set apart a word or phrase within a sentence.

Talking about words and letters

Quotation marks are used when **words themselves** are being discussed in writing:

> *I think there should be a comma between 'it' and 'and'.*
>
> *He had to check how to spell 'Mississippi'.*

Quotation marks may also be used when discussing individual letters:

> *Is there an 'e' in your surname?*
>
> *She had difficulty in pronouncing the letter 'r'.*

An alternative method, which is used in this book, is to use italics when talking about words or letters themselves.

Scare quotes

Quotation marks are also used to mark off words when the writer wants, for one reason or another, to distance himself or herself from the writing. Quotation marks used in this way are sometimes referred to as 'scare quotes'. The word or phrase is not an actual quotation, but may be:

- technical jargon
- slang
- a cliché
- dialect
- a euphemistic term
- an archaic term

The quotation marks are, therefore, a signal to the reader that the writer is not using his or her own voice for what is inside the quotes, or that he or she is being facetious, ironic or sarcastic. (In speech, it is these words that are sometimes accompanied by a gesture in which both index fingers are crooked to indicate inverted commas.) Here are some examples:

> *Apparently, the object of these sessions was to encourage us to 'get in touch with our feelings'.*

> *Smith expected to receive a 'bung' whenever a player was transferred.*

> *Quotation marks used in this way are sometimes referred to as 'scare quotes'.*

The use of quotation marks to indicate titles
Traditionally, the titles of books, plays, articles and poems were enclosed in quotation marks:

> *My brother is a huge fan of 'The Lord of the Rings'.*

> *She gave a fine performance as Rosalind in 'As You Like It'.*

This method is still sometimes used in handwritten texts, but elsewhere it is now more common to italicize titles.

QUOTATION MARKS

In academic writing, the usual style is to use quotation marks for minor titles, such as those of articles in journals and magazines, unpublished essays and dissertations, and the titles of chapters or sections of books, whereas italics are used for major titles, such as those of books, plays, poems, films, newspapers and periodicals:

> She had written a pessimistic article in a local magazine ('Toolmakers Face the Axe', *Rutland Gazette*, March 2004).

> I was reading a fascinating piece in *Cheese Today* entitled 'Swiss Cheese: The Hole Truth'.

> 'The Force of Circumstance' is included in the first volume of his *Collected Short Stories*.

Single and double quotation marks

There are two types of quotation mark: **single quotes** ('...') and **double quotes** ("..."). The standard conventions surrounding these are as follows:

- For enclosing direct speech and quotations, either single or double quotes may be used, but British style tends to favour single quotes.
- For other uses, only single quotation marks should be used.

Advantages of using single quotation marks for quoting speech

If you are using single quotation marks and there is a second quotation embedded within the first one, the first quotation is marked off by single quotes, and the embedded quotation is marked off by double quotes, as in:

> *The assistant manager declared, 'These are "circumstances beyond my individual control", as Mr Micawber said.'*

The first set of quotation marks separates off all the words actually spoken by the assistant manager. However, he has used not only his own words, but also those of Mr Micawber (a character in Charles Dickens' *David Copperfield*). The use of the two different types of quotation marks allows the embedded speech to be differentiated.

Disadvantages of using single quotation marks for quoting speech

The preference for single rather than double quotation marks can cause difficulties in two sets of circumstances.

The first of these is when there is an apostrophe inside the quotation. Look at the following example:

> *As Lillian Hellman said, 'I cannot and will not cut my conscience to suit this year's fashions.'*

This doesn't create too much of a problem. But, look at the next example:

> *She opined, 'Dickens' female characters were either hags or angels, and, as was so often the case, women were the victims of male writers' prejudices, caricatured or idealized.'*

The reader could be forgiven for being at something of a loss to know where the quote ends. If double quotes were used here, no such confusion would arise:

> *She opined, "Dickens' female characters were either hags or angels, and, as was so often the case, women were the victims of male writers' prejudices, caricatured or idealized."*

The second problem relates to the highlighting function of quotation marks, where only single (never double) quotes are used. If a highlighted word appears within a quotation marked off by single quotation marks, the reader might find it difficult to see where the quote begins or ends:

> *'Of course, 'poverty' and 'hardship' no longer mean what they did fifty years ago,' she said.*

Again, double quotes make it easier to interpret the meaning:

> *"Of course, 'poverty' and 'hardship' no longer mean what they did fifty years ago," she said.*

Checklist

1. **The use of quotation marks to enclose speech and quotations**
   - to enclose the exact words used by the speaker or writer being quoted
   - not used for indirect speech or quotations

2. **The use of quotation marks to highlight words in a sentence**
   - when talking about words or letters
   - to create a distance between the writer and the words – 'scare quotes'

3. **The use of quotation marks to indicate titles**
   - used for titles as an alternative to italics
   - in academic writing, to indicate minor titles, eg of articles in a periodical

4. **Single and double quotation marks**
   - either single or double marks may be used for speech and quotations
   - for other uses, only single quotation marks should be used

Punctuation in practice

The following sentences should have some part enclosed in quotation marks. Where should the quotation marks go?

1 *It was in this film that the character played by Michael Douglas famously said, Lunch is for wimps.*

2 *Are we there yet? asked Bart.*

3 *I am pretty sure, said Pete, that it will be ready before Saturday.*

4 *I don't use the words absolute genius lightly.*

5 *Next week we'll examine the stream of consciousness technique in greater detail, the tutor announced.*

6 *They spoke a very archaic form of English full of thous and thees.*

Brackets

i

There are four different kinds of **brackets**: round brackets ( ), square brackets [ ], brace brackets { } and angle brackets < >. Brackets are sometimes called **parentheses**.

The function of brackets

The broad function of brackets is to enclose additional information that is less important than the other information in a sentence or passage. Brackets are a useful way of adding information without interfering too much with the reader's concentration on the sense of what appears before and after them. Brackets isolate information more effectively than a pair of commas would. More specifically, round brackets are used in the following ways:

- to include a **clarification or explanation of what has gone before**, as in the following examples:

    The phenomenon of 'sundowning' (wearing down at the end of the day) can be observed in many patients.

    New targets were set for the growth of the money supply M1 (the amount of cash in circulation plus deposits in cheque accounts).

- to give **additional or incidental information**, as in:

    Walter Camp (1859–1925) is regarded as the father of American football.

    Senator Nuñez (Democrat, Arizona) made a stirring speech.

- to enclose a **personal comment by the writer**, as in:

    Camping (not everyone's cup of tea) is a relatively inexpensive option.

    My (admittedly rather amateurish) effort was rejected out of hand.

- to include **examples**, as in:

    Many types of shellfish (for example, mussels and oysters) can be farmed quite readily given the correct conditions.

    Several clubs (including Ajax, Milan and Barcelona) were reported to be interested in signing him.

- to **identify or specify**, as in:

    Economists predict that growth will slow down in the G8 countries (United States, Russia, Canada, Japan, Britain, France, Germany and Italy) over the next five years.

    In their winter plumage, the redshank (Tringa totanus) and the spotted redshank (Tringa erythropus) are virtually indistinguishable.

- to enclose an **abbreviation** following the full form, where the abbreviated form will be used again later in the text, as in:

    Bovine spongiform encephalopathy (BSE) should therefore be eradicated from British herds by this date. There have been no reported cases of BSE in grass-fed herds.

- to show **equivalents or translations**, as in:

    Temperatures will fall to 15°C (59°F) in the late evening.

    His most important plays include L'École des femmes (The School for Wives) and L'Avare (The Miser).

- to enclose a **reference** to another part of the text or to other texts, as in:

  The colon is sometimes followed by a dash (see Chapter 10) when it introduces a tabulated list.

  I read her piece ('Toolmakers Face the Axe', Rutland Gazette, March 2004) with some amazement.

- as a **space-saving method of indicating options**, as in:

  Any objection(s) should be made in writing to the Planning Department.

  If anyone is interested in applying, (s)he should notify a committee member.

- to enclose **numbers or letters that highlight points within a sentence**, as in:

  Their declared aims and objectives were: (a) to bring the company back to profitability within two years, and (b) to exploit new overseas markets.

Note that where the number or letter is used to mark off a section or paragraph, the opening bracket is usually omitted, as in:

  1) Co-operative ventures.

  2) New product lines.

  3) Resources and staffing.

When brackets should not be used

Brackets should not be used unnecessarily to insert a complete sentence inside another, as in:

  ✗ *UN troops (all units are commanded by an officer experienced in peacekeeping duties) have been deployed along the ceasefire line.*

Instead, the commenting sentence should follow the primary sentence and should start with a capital letter and end with a full stop, as in:

> ✔ *UN troops have been deployed along the ceasefire line. All units are commanded by an officer experienced in peace-keeping duties.*

Alternatively, the comment should be reworded to integrate it more fully into the surrounding sentence, as in:

> ✔ *UN troops, all units of which are commanded by an officer experienced in peacekeeping duties, have been deployed along the ceasefire line.*

Some important points relating to the use of brackets

Brackets come in pairs
Remember that brackets come in pairs, except where a closing bracket is used after a number in a list. Don't forget to add the closing bracket, especially when the bracketed information extends over more than one line.

Brackets should not stand alone at the beginning or end of a line
An opening bracket should never stand on its own at the end of a line, nor should a closing bracket appear at the beginning of a line. There must be at least one word following an opening bracket before the text goes over to the next line, and at least one word preceding a closing bracket at the start of a new line.

Brackets and punctuation
Punctuation that belongs to the information that appears within the brackets should always be included within the brackets and not outside them.

A full stop should not be used after bracketed material that is inserted into a sentence, although there may be a question mark or an exclamation mark, as in:

> *Old Grumpy (wouldn't you have guessed?) has been making all our lives miserable.*

> *His record collection (everything from Abba to ZZ Top!) is meticulously catalogued.*

Where bracketed information comes at the end of a sentence, the full stop comes after the last bracket.

> *He was born in Sofia, but grew up in Constantinople (now Istanbul).*

Multiple sets of brackets

Sometimes, it is necessary to have one pair of brackets inside another pair, as in:

> *The father of Alexander the Great (Philip II (382–336 BC) king of Macedon) organized the Greek states in a federal league, with himself as their general.*

For the sake of clarity, however, you should try to avoid having one pair of brackets nested inside another pair like this. Moreover, an opening or closing bracket should not immediately follow another opening or closing bracket, unless the particular structure of the text makes this completely unavoidable:

> ✗ *The father of Alexander the Great (Philip II, king of Macedon (382–336 BC)) organized the Greek states in a federal league, with himself as their general.*

Square brackets, braces and angle brackets

Besides the more familiar 'round' brackets, you may also come across three other types of bracket:

Square brackets [ ]

Square brackets are used to enclose comments, corrections, explanations and queries introduced into another person's words by the writer or editor:

> *'My mother [the film director Lise Jaspersen] was a huge influence on my career,' she says.*
>
> *Torrance was upbeat about the project. 'I think that having Janet [Simpkins] on board will make a big difference to us,' he said.*

Square brackets also enclose the Latin word *sic* (which literally means 'thus'), which is used to indicate that the quoted passage contains an error or unconventional construction which the writer has not attempted to correct:

> *One of the applicants claimed to have 'an unspeakable [sic] grasp of English spelling'.*

Braces { }

The brace symbols appear on most computer keyboards but are not used in standard English punctuation. They are found in technical fields, such as in mathematics and formal logic, which need not concern us in this book.

Angle brackets < >

Like braces, angle brackets appear on the standard keyboard, but are not used in standard English punctuation. They have some uses in technical fields, such as in computing and textual criticism, which need not concern us in this book.

> *Usage*
>
> In normal writing, do not attempt to use square brackets, braces or angle brackets as a substitute for normal 'round' brackets.

BRACKETS

Checklist

1. **The function of brackets**
   - to enclose additional information that is less important than the other information in a sentence or passage

2. **When brackets should not be used**
   - to insert a complete sentence inside another

3. **Some important points relating to the use of brackets**
   - brackets come in pairs: don't forget to include the closing bracket
   - brackets should not stand alone at the beginning or end of a line
   - punctuation that belongs to bracketed information should be included within the brackets
   - try to avoid having one pair of brackets inside another pair

4. **Square brackets, braces and angle brackets**
   - these have special uses, and are not interchangeable with round brackets

Punctuation in practice

The following sentences should have some part enclosed in brackets. Where should the brackets go?

1. *His wife odd as it may seem is a keep-fit instructor.*

2. *The house sparrow Passer domesticus has grey and brown plumage.*

3. *The use of bleaches is explained in Chapter 10 pages 56–62.*

4. *Her collection includes records from the 1960s for example Marvin Gaye, The Shadows and Dusty Springfield as well as more recent music.*

5. *Jerry has a passion for Italian cheeses eg Pecorino and Mozzarella, but also enjoys some British cheeses eg Double Gloucester and Red Leicester.*

The dash

i

The **dash** can be written as a short line (–) or a long line (—), and is used either as a separating, linking or substituting device.

The dash as a separating device

The dash may be used to separate off parts of a sentence (functioning in much the same way as a pair of commas or a pair of brackets). As a separating device, the dash is used in several ways.

Additional comments

A dash can be used to mark off an explanation, comment or aside that has been inserted into a sentence. Note that if the comment or explanation comes in the middle of the sentence, a **pair of dashes** must be used; if it comes at the end of the sentence, it is preceded by a single dash. Here are some examples:

> *The appearance of the wood – the colour, the texture and the grain pattern – is the most important consideration when choosing the material for any woodworking project.*

> *Western influence is apparent as you walk the streets of the capital – Starbuck's, hamburger joints and Friends on TV.*

> *He told me once – believe it if you will – that he had climbed every mountain in the French Alps.*

> *He had climbed every mountain in the French Alps – or so he claimed.*

Note that a pair of dashes usually signals an interruption that is stronger or more emphatic than one marked by a pair of commas, but not as strong as one marked by a pair of brackets.

Summing up

A dash can be used to show that what follows is a summing up of
what went before. In two-part sentences where a general or
summing-up statement is followed by an itemized or more detailed
explanation, the normal punctuation mark would be a colon, as in:

> *There are some serious drawbacks in this particular
> scheme: its expense, its duration and its severe effects on
> the environment.*

However, if the sentence order is reversed, a dash may be used in
place of the colon, as in:

> *Its expense, its duration and its severe effects on the envi-
> ronment – these are some of the serious drawbacks of this
> particular scheme.*

Emphatic comments

A dash can be used to indicate that what follows has a more
emphatic tone than what has gone before, as in:

> *This bleach kills all known germs – dead.*

A dash can often introduce a pointed remark added at the end of a
sentence, as in:

> *They were impressed by her charming personality, her
> intelligence, her sense of humour – and her money.*

An emphatic comment in the middle of a sentence can be enclosed
by a pair of dashes, as in:

> *Unfortunately, there was nothing – absolutely nothing –
> that we could have done about it.*

Interrupted sentences

A dash is the correct punctuation mark to use when a sentence breaks off in the middle because of an interruption, as in:

> *What really galls me is that he actually believed – oh, but what's the use of going on about it now?*

> *'Whatever you do, don't touch the —' But it was already too late.*

This use of the dash is only appropriate to the kinds of writing in which actual conversation is being represented. It is not usually appropriate for formal writing.

Lists

We saw on page 45 that a colon is the correct punctuation mark to introduce a list. Where each item in the list appears on a new line, a dash is sometimes placed immediately after the colon. This is unnecessary but not wrong:

> *Please assemble in the lobby with the following:–*
>
> > *walking boots*
> >
> > *sandwiches*
> >
> > *flask*
> >
> > *sleeping bag*

However, when the items in the list are not tabulated, but follow the colon on the same line, a dash should not be used between the colon and the first item of the list:

✗ *He grows all sorts of vegetables:– peas, beans, carrots, onions and cauliflower.*

✔ *He grows all sorts of vegetables: peas, beans, carrots, onions and cauliflower.*

The dash as a linking device

The dash may be used to join together similar words and numbers in two particular ways.

Ranges of numbers

A dash is the correct punctuation mark to use to indicate a range of numbers, as in:

> *1914–1918*
>
> *103–105 Oxford Street*
>
> *pages 325–387*

Of course, it is also possible to spell out ranges without using a dash. The last of the examples might be written as *between pages 325 and 387* or *from page 325 to page 387*. Note that when a dash is used, it replaces both the words *between* and *and* in the first structure, and both the words *from* and *to* in the second structure. Avoid using a dash if you have already started to indicate the range by writing *between* or *from*:

- ✗ *There were between 25–35 vehicles involved in the collision.*

- ✗ *She lived there from 1967–68.*

- ✔ *There were between 25 and 35 vehicles involved in the collision.*

- ✔ *There were 25–35 vehicles involved in the collision.*

- ✔ *She lived there from 1967 to 1968.*

Linking words of equal importance

A dash is the correct punctuation mark to use to link two or more words of equal importance, as in:

> *Marsha was keen to establish a good pupil–teacher relationship.*

The Lions won by a score of 45–10.

More delays are expected on the Glasgow–Edinburgh line.

We were hoping for a France–Croatia final.

> **Usage**
>
> In these cases, you could equally use a slash between the two items, but the dash is more appropriate for formal writing.

The dash as a substituting device

A dash can be used to avoid spelling out a swearword or expletive that may cause offence to readers. The normal way of doing this is to write only the first letter of the word you do not wish to spell out and use the dash to replace the remaining letters:

Charlie was thrown out for calling the landlord a f—ing yokel.

Nowadays, this technique is only used for the most extreme and taboo swearwords and expletives. However, it is interesting to note that the technique of using a dash to replace parts of such words led to the formation of new milder forms of the original words: for example, *Damn it!* was often written *D— it!*, which led to the phrase *Dash it!*; and, more recently, *F— off!* has produced the euphemism *Eff off!*

En dashes and em dashes

For the real punctuation aficionado, it is worth noting that a dash can appear in two different lengths. A short dash is about twice the length of a hyphen (-) and is known as an **en dash** or **en rule**. There is also another dash that is twice as long again (—). This is known as the **em dash** or **em rule**. ('Em' and 'en' are terms used in printing for measuring type, an en being half an em. The terms come from the fact that the letter 'em' takes up twice as much space as the letter 'en' in a printed book.)

THE DASH

In practical terms, the differences between the en dash and the em dash are as follows:

- Where an em dash is used, it is closed up to any words that come before and after. However, if an en dash is used, there is a space before and after the dash.
- Either an em or en dash may be used as a separating device, although, the em dash is used less commonly nowadays.
- Only an en dash can be used as a linking device.
- An em dash is used as a substituting device.

i

There is no key for a dash on a standard keyboard. In typed texts, the en dash is often represented by two hyphens (–), and the em dash by three hyphens (—). If you are using a computer, you can create an en dash (provided the 'Num Lock' feature is turned on) by holding down the 'Alt' key and typing 0150. Holding down the 'Alt' key and typing 0151 creates the longer em dash. However, if you just enter a hyphen with a space on either side of it, the computer will often change this automatically to an en dash.

Dashes and hyphens

The dash should be distinguished from the hyphen, which is a shorter line. The hyphen is dealt with on pages 78–86.

Checklist

1. **The dash as a separating device**
- for comments inserted into a sentence
- to introduce a summing up of what has gone before
- to mark emphatic comments
- when a sentence breaks off in the middle because of an interruption
- immediately after the colon when introducing a tabulated list

2. **The dash as a linking device**
- to express a range of numbers
- to join terms of equal importance

3. **The dash as a substituting device**
- to avoid spelling out an offensive word

4. **En dashes and em dashes**
- both types of dash can be used as separating devices
- en dashes can also be used as linking devices
- em dashes can also be used as substituting devices

5. **Dashes and hyphens**
- don't confuse these punctuation marks

Punctuation in practice

These sentences each contain a short phrase that may be enclosed by either a pair of round brackets or a pair of dashes. Add the appropriate punctuation marks to each. Note that there may also be missing commas in some of the sentences:

1 *A majority of those polled on Tuesday and Wednesday 55% and 57% respectively do not believe the president should resign.*

2 *Josh or Nick I'm not sure which will pick you up from the station tomorrow.*

3 *In his attempt to secure the succession for his strongly Protestant daughter-in-law Warwick now duke of Northumberland failed dismally.*

The slash

The **slash** (/) is also called the **oblique**, the **solidus**, the **stroke** or the **virgule**.

Use of the slash to separate alternatives

A slash can be used to separate two or more items when it is not known which one applies, or when any could apply, as in:

Dear Sir/Madam

Please write your credit card/debit card/bank account number below.

The athletes will each have his/her own room in the Olympic village. When s/he has finished his/her particular event or training for the day, he/she will have a place to relax.

In more formal writing the slash can usually be replaced by the word *or*.

Use of the slash in abbreviated forms

A slash is used in certain short forms, usually where there is a word-break between two abbreviations, as in:

Replies should be sent to Fraser Hamilton, c/o [= care of] Brown, 47 Appleyard Drive, Oxford.

Suggs was appointed officer i/c [= in charge of] supplies.

Use of the slash in dates

A slash can be used between two dates or partial dates to indicate a period of time, as in:

> *This assessment applies to the 2004/5 tax year.*
>
> *He has announced that he will retire at the end of the 2006/7 season.*

Use of the slash in rates and ratios

A slash can be used instead of the word 'per' in expressions that indicate a rate or ratio, as in:

> *a top speed of 250 km/h* [= 250 kilometres per hour]

Use of the slash to link items

A slash can be used as a more informal alternative to a short en dash to link items of equal importance, especially places on a route, as in:

> *The Manchester/Newark/San Francisco flight has been cancelled.*
>
> *Andy had tickets to the Arsenal/Chelsea game.*

The slash in website addresses

A slash is also used to mark off a part of the address of a site on the World Wide Web that can be accessed from the previous level of the address, as in:

> *Tom was advised to check out www.feline-world.org/advice.*
>
> *For full details of the post, see www.goldmine.com/marketing/opportunities.*

1. **Use of the slash to separate alternatives**
- when it is not known which one applies, or when any could apply

2. **Use of the slash in abbreviated forms**
- in some short forms, such as *c/o* and *a/c*

3. **Use of the slash in dates**
- to indicate a period of time

4. **Use of the slash in rates and ratios**
- to mean *per*

5. **Use of the slash to link items**
- to link items of equal importance, especially places on a route

6. **The slash in website addresses**
- to mark off different levels in a web address

Punctuation in practice

Insert a slash in the appropriate place in these sentences:

1 *This car can't manage much more than 80 kmh.*
2 *They talked about recording an old Lennon McCartney song.*
3 *Your ticket will expire at the end of the 2010 2011 season.*
4 *Didn't I see you on the London York train?*
5 *Please bring your passport proof of identity with you.*

i

The **hyphen** (-) is a short line used to link words or parts of words.

The function of the hyphen

The basic function of the hyphen is to join together words or parts of words to show that they are to be read as a single unit:

> *The hotel is advertised as being dog-friendly.*
>
> *He is a well-known figure around these parts.*
>
> *This film has a strong anti-racist message.*

When is a hyphen necessary?

There often seems to be little logic or consistency in the hyphenation of words in English. The reason for this is that there are few 'rules' as such – hyphenation is often a question of style and common sense, rather than a matter of principle. The modern tendency is to use a hyphen only when it is strictly necessary, with the result that written texts have much less hyphenation than used to be the case. A text peppered with unnecessary hyphens now tends to look both fussy and old-fashioned, and it is desirable to avoid hyphens as much as possible. There are, however, a few fixed rules that should be followed regarding the use of hyphens.

Clarity

The first and most important of these general rules is that a hyphen should always be used when clarity demands it. Keep in mind that the only way that we can indicate in writing the stress patterns used in speech is to use appropriate punctuation. Hyphenation has an important role in this respect. Compare the following examples:

> *He has twenty-odd cousins.*
>
> *He has twenty odd cousins.*

If the intended sense here is 'He has twenty or more cousins' rather than 'He has twenty cousins who are peculiar in some way', the hyphen should not be omitted.

Units of more than two words

For some nouns that are constructed out of more than two words, hyphens are often the only way that the words may be linked effectively, as in:

> *a will-o'-the-wisp*
>
> *a johnny-come-lately*
>
> *a ne'er-do-well*
>
> *father-in-law*

Here, it is obviously not possible to make a single word out of the elements of the phrase. Furthermore, if the words are not connected by hyphens it would make these phrases more difficult to read when they crop up in a sentence:

> *Karl was a johnny come lately to the joys of family life.*

Note, however, that phrases that function as nouns are not hyphenated where the individual words still retain their independent force:

> *the balance of payments*
>
> *an environmental health officer*

Units of two or more words that come in front of a noun

Hyphens should be used in phrases made up of two or more words when these are used like adjectives and come before a noun, as in:

> *the balance-of-payments deficit*
>
> *a happy-go-lucky character*
>
> *a zero-tolerance approach*
>
> *a first-class ticket*
>
> *a long-standing feud*
>
> *a two-or-more-word unit*

Note, however, that when phrases like this follow the noun, they are **not** hyphenated, as in:

> *a deficit in the balance of payments*
>
> *a feud of long standing*
>
> *a unit of two or more words*

When a hyphen should not be used

Two-word noun phrases

It is unnecessary to add a hyphen in a phrase consisting of two separate words whose meaning is perfectly clear without a hyphen. Here are some examples of phrases that should not be hyphenated:

> *false teeth*
>
> *a fashion victim*
>
> *a mortise lock*
>
> *a putting green*
>
> *a root vegetable*

> *a violin concerto*
>
> *a plumber's mate*

Adverbs ending in -ly

We have seen that the general rule is that hyphens should be used in phrases made up of two or more words when these are used like adjectives and come before a noun. However, when the first word of the unit is an adverb ending in *-ly*, there is usually no hyphen between the adverb and adjective, as in:

> *a beautifully kept garden*
>
> *a greatly enlarged illustration*
>
> *abnormally sensitive gums*
>
> *he and his equally snobbish wife*

There are a few exceptions to the *-ly* rule. These occur when the adverb ending in *-ly* is so closely linked with the following word that the pair is regarded as a fixed expression, as in:

> *a highly-strung pony*
>
> *a fully-fledged member of the aristocracy*

The use of the hyphen in compound words

Many standard English words have been formed by joining together two separate words. For example, *cowshed* is formed from *cow* and *shed*, and *wristwatch* from *wrist* and *watch*. Words that have been formed in this way are known as 'compound words'.

Compound nouns

There is often doubt about whether a compound noun such as *cowshed* should be written as one word, as two words (*cow shed*), or with a hyphen (*cow-shed*). In many cases, all three versions are acceptable, but the modern style is not to write compound nouns with a hyphen unless one is absolutely necessary. There are two main reasons why a hyphen might be required when writing a compound noun:

- A hyphen is used if it avoids a visually unacceptable combination of letters (*cliff-face*, *cross-stitch*), or if a reader might well misread the word if it appeared as a single unit (*hip-hop*, *sun-up*).
- Compounds that are still thought of as being the sum of their parts rather than recognized as a single concept are often hyphenated. The hyphen is often dropped as the one-word compound becomes more familiar. It is interesting to note that many relatively new compound nouns were originally written with hyphens (*air-bag*, *hot-line*, *web-site*). However, as they have become recognized as familiar concepts and not just as the sum of their parts, it has become customary to write these as a single word (*airbag*, *hotline*, *website*).

Compound verbs

When a two-word compound is used as a verb, it is written with a hyphen if the second element carries the force of the verb, as in:

> She tends to clock-watch as five o'clock approaches.
>
> They like to water-ski in their spare time.
>
> The village was carpet-bombed.

However, a hyphen is not used for 'phrasal verbs', in which the verb element comes before another word:

> He certainly takes after his father.
>
> She comes across as being rather pushy.

The use of the hyphen after prefixes

A prefix is a group of letters that does not constitute a word in its own right, but which can be added to the beginning of another word to modify its meaning. By and large, words that are formed using prefixes are written as single words without hyphens. Thus, you would write *cooperate*, *regroup*, *subhuman* and *unable* rather than *co-operate*, *re-group*, *sub-human* and *un-able*.

However, when the addition of a prefix might create confusion with another word, a hyphen is often inserted to make the meaning clear:

> *After ten years, they decided to re-form* [not *reform*] *the band.*

> *I asked them to send someone to re-lay* [not *relay*] *the carpet.*

Similarly, if the addition of the prefix without a hyphen produces a difficult-to-read combination of letters, a hyphen is required:

✔ *sources of non-nuclear energy*

✘ *sources of nonnuclear energy*

When a prefix is added to a hyphenated compound, a hyphen must also be added between the prefix and the first word of the compound, as in:

> *his pre-university-lecturing days*

A hyphen is also required when the first letter of the word to which the prefix is attached has a capital letter, as in:

> *anti-American protests*

> *the pre-Christian era*

> *post-Reformation art*

The use of the hyphen to split words at the end of a line

Another use of the hyphen is to split a word when the whole word will not fit at the end of a written line. This use of the hyphen is common in printed texts and is illustrated in the following example:

> He has often encountered a great deal of opposition from local residents.

Usage

For word splits at the ends of lines, it is important to remember that the hyphen should always appear at the end of the first line, and never at the beginning of the second.

Where possible, it is better to avoid splitting words at the ends of lines, but when this is unavoidable, the split should be made in a way that causes minimum interruption to the flow of the text. Follow these do's and don'ts on splitting words at the ends of lines:

- Don't split words of five or fewer letters.
- Do try to split longer words at a place where there is a break between syllables (*keep-sake* rather than *ke-epsake*; *mile-stone* rather than *mi-lestone*). The word should, ideally, be split somewhere in the middle so that it is more or less equally divided between the first and second line.
- Do split words to avoid the possibility that the word may be mispronounced or read as a whole word on the first line (*re-install* rather than *rein-stall*; *ther-apist* rather than *the-rapist*).
- Don't split a word in any way that may cause the reader to hesitate or re-read the split word in order to follow the sense.
- If a word would naturally be written with a hyphen (as in *pre-Christian* or *father-in-law*), don't split it anywhere other than at that hyphen.

Hyphens and dashes

The hyphen should be distinguished from the dash, which is a longer line. The dash is dealt with on pages 67–74.

Checklist

1. The function of the hyphen
- to join together words or parts of words to show that they are to be read as a single unit

2. When is a hyphen necessary?
- when the meaning would not be clear without it
- for some units of more than two words that function as a noun
- for units of two or more words that stand in front of a noun

3. When a hyphen should not be used
- in phrases consisting of two separate words whose meaning is perfectly clear without a hyphen
- for units of two or more words when the first word ends in *-ly*

4. The use of the hyphen in compound words
- avoid hyphens in compound nouns, unless they are required to avoid an awkward combination of letters or the word is thought of as the sum of its parts
- compound verbs are written with a hyphen if the second element of the compound is a verb

5. The use of the hyphen after prefixes
- when the addition of a prefix would create confusion with another word
- when it avoids an awkward grouping of letters
- when a prefix is added to a hyphenated compound
- when the word to which the prefix is attached begins with a capital letter

6. The use of the hyphen to split words at the end of a line
- the split should be made in a way that causes minimum interruption to the flow of the text

- split words at a place where there is a break between syllables
- do not split a word in any way that may cause the reader to hesitate or re-read the split word in order to follow the sense

7. **Hyphens and dashes**
- do not confuse these punctuation marks

Punctuation in practice

Insert a hyphen in the appropriate place in these sentences:

1 *Harry is a top class performer on the cello.*

2 *She was sitting on a bench eating a fried egg sandwich.*

3 *Jane was selected to ice skate in the Olympics.*

4 *Heffernan chipped in with three second half goals.*

5 *This book has been printed on acid free paper.*

Part Two

Putting Punctuation to Use

Which punctuation mark?

It is all very well to know what the different punctuation marks are, but sometimes it is not obvious which punctuation mark is the right one to use in a particular place. This chapter addresses some of the situations where uncertainty can arise.

Full stop, question mark or exclamation mark?

It is sometimes not immediately obvious whether it is correct to use a full stop, an exclamation mark or a question mark at the end of a sentence.

If you are not sure which to use, keep in mind the principle that the correct punctuation mark to use is the one that matches the underlying **meaning** of the sentence, rather than the one that might be suggested by its **form**.

For example, some requests are presented in the grammatical form of a question, but they are not in fact meant as questions, and they would be spoken with a level intonation, rather than with the rising intonation that indicates a question. These requests should be written with a full stop, as in:

> *Would all students who want to take study leave please give their details as soon as possible to a staff member in the school office.*
>
> *Could you pass me the salt and pepper, please.*
>
> *Would you kindly accompany me to the station.*

WHICH PUNCTUATION MARK?

However, if there is some doubt about whether a request will be complied with, it is correct to use a question mark:

> *Could you send me that letter by tomorrow, please?*
>
> *Could you possibly accompany me to the station?*

As we saw on page 16, many sentences that are written in the form of questions are in fact exclamations and not requests for information. These should be written with an exclamation mark, as in:

> *What on earth are you doing!*   [= I am amazed at what you are doing]

Again, if there is a genuine request for information involved, it is correct to use a question mark:

> *What on earth are you doing?*   [= I want to know what you are doing]

Exclamation marks should be used sparingly (see page 18), and a full stop is usually sufficient to express a command or an emphatic or humorous statement, unless you are recording actual speech:

> *Please send me the results tomorrow.*
>
> *Judging from the way he drives, he seems to think he is Michael Schumacher.*

Remember, also, that a full stop should be used when a question is reported indirectly rather than being quoted word for word:

✔ *Jerry asked Tom if he wanted to go to the party.*

✘ *Jerry asked Tom if he wanted to go to the party?*

Similarly, a full stop should be used when a command or exclamation is reported indirectly:

✔ *She told him to hurry up and get out of the bathroom.*

✘ *She told him to hurry up and get out of the bathroom!*

Full stop, comma or semicolon?

When two statements are related to one another, there is sometimes a doubt as to whether to use a full stop, a comma or a semicolon to separate them.

If you have two complete statements with **no connecting word or words** between them, they can be joined either by a full stop or a semicolon. If you use a full stop, the second statement must begin with a capital letter:

✔ *Colin will be twelve in September. His brother is two years younger.*

If you want to show that the two statements are connected, you can use a semicolon instead of a full stop. If you use a semicolon, the second statement is part of the same sentence, so it does not begin with a capital letter:

✔ *Colin will be twelve in September; his brother is two years younger.*

If there is **a connecting word** such as *and* or *but* between the two statements, then it is correct to separate the two statements with a comma, and a full stop is required only at the end of the connected statements:

✔ *Colin will be twelve in September, but his brother is two years younger.*

It is incorrect to use a comma when there is no connecting word between the two statements:

✘ *Colin will be twelve in September, his brother is two years younger.*

WHICH PUNCTUATION MARK?

If there is a connecting word such as *however* or *nevertheless*, which not only connects but also comments on the second statement, then it is correct to separate the two statements with a semicolon and add a comma after the connecting word:

✔ *Colin will be twelve in September; however, his brother is two years younger.*

Colon or semicolon?

When there is a strong break between the two parts of a sentence, you might judge that something more powerful than a comma is required. Two available punctuation marks are the colon and the semicolon. Does it matter which you use?

If one part **expands on, explains** or **completes** the other, a colon is the correct punctuation mark, as in:

> *We all burst out laughing: Vic was doing one of his impressions.*

> *There are three important things about a house: location, location and location.*

However, if one part **balances** or **contrasts** with the other (rather than expanding, explaining or completing it), a semicolon is the correct punctuation mark, as in:

> *To err is human; to forgive, divine.*

> *There were scowls and sneers from the two sisters; there were blushes and giggles from their friends.*

Note the difference in meaning that the two marks can create. The semicolon in the following sentence suggests that the two statements are balanced, and Frankie's laughter and Jim's embarrassment both arise independently from the same source:

> *Frankie laughed hysterically; Jim was turning purple with embarrassment.*

If a colon is used, the second statement should be read as an explanation of the first, with the implication that Frankie's laughter arises from Jim's embarrassment:

> *Frankie laughed hysterically: Jim was turning purple with embarrassment.*

Brackets, dashes or commas?

> **i**
> Extra information that is inserted into a sentence that is already complete in itself is called a **parenthesis** or **parenthetic information**.

When you want to mark off 'parenthetic' information within a sentence, you can use brackets, dashes or commas. The choice depends on how much you want to distance the parenthetic information from the rest of the sentence.

Brackets are the strongest way to mark off parenthetic information. They are used around information that is less important than the surrounding sentence. The words inside the brackets do not have to flow as smoothly from what went before as the words enclosed by dashes or commas:

> *Camping (not everyone's cup of tea) is a relatively inexpensive option.*

Dashes also represent a strong break, often suggesting a change in emphasis or tone from the surrounding sentence. However, they are not as strong as brackets, and the words inside the dashes should flow on smoothly from what went before:

> *Camping is a relatively inexpensive – albeit much less comfortable – option.*

WHICH PUNCTUATION MARK?

Commas are the weakest form of punctuation for parenthetic information. The words enclosed by commas are not cut off as distinctly from the surrounding sentence:

Camping is, as you might expect, a relatively inexpensive option.

Usage

Note that, whichever punctuation you use, you should place the punctuation so that the sentence will still make sense if it is read with the parenthetic information deleted.

Checklist

1. **Full stop, question mark or exclamation mark?**
   - use the punctuation that matches the underlying meaning, rather than the one that might be suggested by the form of the sentence
   - use a full stop for indirect questions and commands

2. **Full stop, comma or semicolon?**
   - use a full stop or semicolon if there is no connecting word
   - use a comma if there is a simple connecting word
   - use a semicolon if there is a connecting word that also comments on the second statement

3. **Colon or semicolon?**
   - use a colon if the second statement expands on, explains or completes the first
   - use a semicolon if the two statements are balanced or contrasted

4. **Brackets, dashes or commas?**
   - the choice depends on how strong a break you want: brackets signify the strongest break; commas the weakest

Punctuation in practice

Add punctuation to the following sentences:

1 *Luis asked me if I had ever visited South America*

2 *Can you all give your names to the officer*

3 *I am a keen tennis player but my husband prefers to play golf*

4 *Jared is Capricorn Dylan is a Libra*

5 *Sonya remembered why she hated this place it was too cold*

6 *My brother is it pains me to say more successful than I am*

7 *Strawberries are in my opinion much nicer than raspberries*

Punctuating speech and quotations

Basic principles

The punctuation associated with speech and quotations poses some special questions and is worth considering in detail. Here are the basic principles to follow when recording quotations:

- Quotation marks are placed only around words that are recorded in the exact form in which they were spoken or written.
- Punctuation marks that belong to, or are part of, the quoted speech or writing should be kept within the quotation marks.
- Punctuation that belongs to the surrounding sentence goes outside the quotation marks.
- When quoted words form a complete sentence they start with a capital letter, even if they do not come right at the start of the sentence in which they are included.
- When quoted words do not form a complete sentence they start with a lower-case letter, unless they come right at the start of the sentence in which they are included.

Punctuation at the end of the sentence

We saw on page 6 that when quoting a complete sentence, the closing full stop comes *inside* the closing quotation mark. It is not necessary to add a second full stop outside the closing quotation mark:

✔ *Jerry said regretfully, 'We seem to be out of cheese.'*

✘ *Jerry said regretfully, 'We seem to be out of cheese.'.*

Similarly, if the words inside the quotation marks are a question, the question mark comes inside the closing quotation mark. It is not necessary to add a full stop after the closing quotation mark:

✔ *Jerry looked around and asked, 'Who would like some cheese?'*

✘ *Jerry looked around and asked, 'Who would like some cheese?'.*

If the words inside the quotation marks are an exclamation, the exclamation mark comes inside the closing quotation mark. It is not necessary to add a full stop after the closing quotation mark:

✔ *Jerry gave a satisfied smile and exclaimed, 'I do love cheese!'*

✘ *Jerry gave a satisfied smile and exclaimed, 'I do love cheese!'.*

Note, however, that – unlike full stops – question marks and exclamation marks should not be omitted when there is another sentence marker at the end of a quoted sentence. It is correct to have a question mark or exclamation mark after the closing quotation mark:

✔ *Have you any idea who said, 'When the going gets tough, the tough get going'?*

Here, the question mark belongs to the words *Have you any idea who said* and not to the quoted speech, so it must come after the closing quotation mark. The full stop that would naturally appear at the end of the quotation has given way to the question mark as a sentence marker.

When neither the surrounding sentence nor the quoted sentence naturally ends in a full stop, you may occasionally have two sentence markers:

✔ *He even had the cheek to ask, 'Can I have some more?'!*

✔ *Did I hear you say, 'Can I have some more?'?*

In this last example, the two question marks give the sentence a rather clumsy appearance. It would be more elegant to rephrase it as an indirect question in order to avoid this clash:

Did I hear you ask whether you could have some more?

Punctuation in the middle of the sentence

Before the quotation

When the quoted speech comes after a phrase indicating saying, wondering, etc, it is usually introduced by a comma:

Jerry said regretfully, 'We seem to be out of cheese.'

It is acceptable to use a colon before the opening quotation mark when the quoted speech has the effect of elaborating or expanding on what has gone before the colon, as in:

She told me the last thing I wanted to hear: 'We've all got to go on a team-building course.'

However, when the quoted speech does not expand on what was said before, you should use a comma rather than a colon:

✗ *Ronald Reagan said: 'I can tell a lot about a fellow's character by the way he eats jelly beans.'*

✔ *Ronald Reagan said, 'I can tell a lot about a fellow's character by the way he eats jelly beans.'*

After the quotation

When the quoted speech comes before a phrase indicating saying, wondering, etc, the full stop at the end of the quoted speech is replaced by a comma:

✔ *'We seem to be out of cheese,' said Jerry regretfully.*

✘ *'We seem to be out of cheese.' said Jerry regretfully.*

Note that the comma only replaces a full stop. If the quoted speech ends in a question mark or exclamation mark, a comma is not required:

> *'Are we out of cheese?' asked Jerry.*

Interrupting the quotation

When the quoted speech is broken up by a phrase indicating saying, wondering, etc, a pair of commas is inserted to mark off the interruption in the quotation:

> *'We seem', said Jerry regretfully, 'to be out of cheese.'*

The commas are not part of the quoted speech, and have therefore been placed outside the quotation marks.

When commas are used to 'bracket' the interruption in this way, many people prefer to place the first comma inside the first set of quotes, thus:

> *'We seem,' said Jerry regretfully, 'to be out of cheese.'*

This may seem illogical, since the comma is not part of the quotation. People who prefer this style say that it improves the appearance of the text, in that the comma comes immediately after the last letter. Otherwise, the comma 'floats in space'.

It is really a matter of personal preference which method you use, as long as you are consistent throughout any piece of writing. Some writers omit these bracketing commas altogether, but this is not recommended for essay writing or other texts where punctuation may be assessed or marked by someone with a more traditional view of correct punctuation.

The problem does not arise when there is a natural comma at the point where the quotation is interrupted:

> *'We seem, my friends,' said Jerry regretfully, 'to be out of cheese.'*

Here, the first two commas belong to the quoted speech, and thus the second must come within the first closing quote.

Presentation of longer quotations

A quotation that is no more than one sentence long should be incorporated into the surrounding sentence, being placed within quotation marks, as in:

> *Shakespeare describes England as 'this sceptred isle'.*
>
> *As Harold Wilson once said, 'A week is a long time in politics.'*

Note that, in the first example (where the quotation is a short phrase), the full stop comes outside the closing quotation mark. In the second example, the quotation is a full sentence and the full stop comes inside the closing quotation mark.

It is conventional to insert a slash if you are quoting from a poem or lyric and you want to indicate where a line ends:

> *Shakespeare describes England as 'this sceptred isle, / This earth of majesty'.*

When a passage made up of several sentences, or running to more than three lines, is being quoted, it can be treated as a new paragraph, but indented slightly from the left-hand margin. The introductory line is punctuated with a colon, and it is not necessary to enclose the quoted passage with quotation marks:

Nobody has ever surpassed Shakespeare's description of England:

> *This royal throne of kings, this sceptred isle,*
>
> *This earth of majesty, this seat of Mars,*
>
> *This other Eden, demi-paradise,*
>
> *This fortress built by Nature for herself*
>
> *Against infection and the hand of war,*
>
> *This happy breed of men, this little world,*
>
> *This precious stone set in the silver sea ...*

Omission marks (see pages 6–7) are a useful device when quoting longer passages. They allow you to leave out words and even whole sentences from the passage and pick it up again at a later point:

> *When he talked about joining the Navy, I was reminded of the words of Doctor Johnson:*
>
> > *No man will be a sailor who has contrivance enough to get himself into jail; for being in a ship is being in a jail, with the chance of being drowned ... A man in jail has more room, better food, and commonly better company.*

Remember, too, that (as explained on page 65) you can use square brackets to insert a word or comment that was not originally present in the passage, either to complete the grammatical sense, or to add a comment or explanation of your own.

PUNCTUATING SPEECH AND QUOTATIONS

Checklist

1. **Basic principles**
   - quotation marks are placed only around words that are recorded in the exact form in which they were spoken or written
   - punctuation that belongs to the quoted speech should be kept inside the quotation marks; other punctuation should go outside
   - quotations that are complete sentences should start with a capital letter

2. **Punctuation at the end of the sentence**
   - the closing full stop comes *inside* the closing quotation mark when quoting a complete sentence
   - no full stop is required if the quoted speech ends in a question mark or exclamation mark
   - question marks and exclamation marks should not be omitted when there is another sentence marker at the end of a sentence

3. **Punctuation in the middle of the sentence**
   - quoted speech is introduced by a comma or, if the speech explains what has gone before, a colon
   - the full stop at the end of quoted speech is replaced by a comma
   - a pair of commas is inserted to mark off an interruption in the quoted speech

4. **Presentation of longer quotations**
   - a longer quotation can be written as a new paragraph, introduced by a colon, with no quotation marks and slightly indented
   - use omission marks and square brackets respectively if you wish to cut out or insert text

Punctuation in practice

These sentences have been written with quotation marks only. Can you supply the remaining punctuation?

1 *'Do you actually like oysters' Bob enquired*

2 *Was it Peter or Harry who asked 'Will we be paid expenses'*

3 *'Stop making that horrible noise immediately' she bellowed*

4 *John suddenly shouted 'Look out He's got a gun'*

5 *'I was' said Frank 'completely terrified'*

6 *'If you understand the problem' said Amy 'the answer is obvious'*

Using punctuation for effect

In looking at the various punctuation marks and their uses, we have so far been concerned with using punctuation correctly with the aim of making your writing easy to read. However, you can sometimes use punctuation in slightly more creative ways, especially in informal writing. The exclamation mark, question mark, quotation marks and hyphens can all be used to highlight and emphasize words or sentences.

Bear in mind, however, that while this is quite acceptable for personal messages, it is disapproved of in most other contexts, and it should be particularly avoided in formal writing.

Using exclamation marks for effect

In formal writing, the exclamation mark is used sparingly, principally when recording speech. In informal writing, you can use exclamation marks more freely, and you can even use more than one exclamation mark to indicate extreme emotion:

> *The postman delivered your parcel today. Finally!!!*
>
> *Irritated? I was absolutely furious!!!*

Sometimes, in informal writing, you can combine an exclamation mark with a question mark:

> *Is this the best you can do?!*

An exclamation mark inside a pair of brackets can be used within a sentence to draw attention to something that the writer finds surprising, or to indicate a comment that has been inserted by the author, as in:

> *Although he said he quite enjoyed (!) being ill, he was clearly depressed that morning.*

> *Their (frequent!) visits were becoming increasingly irksome.*

Using question marks for effect

Occasionally, more than one question mark is used as a way of signalling very strong feelings, such as indignation. This technique is used especially after 'rhetorical questions', in which the person asking the question does not really expect an answer, as in:

> *Who the hell does she think she is???*

> *Just what sort of operation are we running here???*

Using quotation marks for effect

We saw earlier that you can use quotation marks as 'scare quotes' to highlight a word or phrase that is being used in an unusual way (see pages 54–5). You can use quotation marks in this way to draw attention to a word you are using ironically when you are being humorous or facetious:

> *All the 'wee lassies' were about fifty and obviously no strangers to the biscuit tin.*

> *We stopped for a spot of 'liquid refreshment' at the Dog and Duck.*

> *My boss was happy to write off the expedition as 'market research'.*

Using hyphens for effect

A further way of drawing attention to a word is to use hyphens to separate the individual letters. This is especially done in places when you would slow down if you were speaking to create special emphasis:

>*You have a-l-m-o-s-t worked it out.*
>
>*Please speak v-e-r-y s-l-o-w-l-y.*
>
>*Of course I'm feeling c-c-c-c-c-cold!*

Usage

All these devices will lose their effectiveness if they are used too much. However, they can be effective if used sparingly.

Emoticons

A recent innovation – used principally in e-mail and text messages – is the use of emoticons (also called 'smileys'). These are combinations of punctuation marks – sometimes including other characters – that are used after sentences with the intention of giving an indication of the writer's facial expression or emotions:

>*I'm sitting by the pool with a cool, refreshing drink :-)*
>[= I am happy]
>
>*I hear that Spurs lost again :-(*
>[= I am sad]
>
>*The boss has suddenly called us in for a meeting :-o*
>[= I am shocked]

Usage

Some people find emoticons irritating, so you are advised not to use them unless you are writing to someone who you know will appreciate them.

Checklist

1. **Using exclamation marks for effect**
- use multiple exclamation marks to indicate extreme emotion
- use exclamation marks inside brackets to draw attention to something

2. **Using question marks for effect**
- use multiple question marks to signal very strong feelings, especially after rhetorical questions

3. **Using quotation marks for effect**
- use to draw attention to a word you are using ironically

4. **Using hyphens for effect**
- use to separate the individual letters of a word when you would slow down if you were speaking

5. **Emoticons**
- used to give an indication of the writer's facial expression or emotions

Modern punctuation trends

You may notice that different writers take different approaches to punctuation. Some use a lot of punctuation marks, whereas other writers seem to manage quite happily with relatively few. This is because, although there are some fixed rules, there is also a certain amount of discretion involved in deciding when punctuation is required. Furthermore, fashions in punctuation change over time. This chapter looks at the changing trends in punctuation and explains the methods most commonly followed in modern writing.

> **i**
> The characteristic feature of modern punctuation style is the use of 'open punctuation', which involves using punctuation marks only where they are strictly necessary.

Commas

Older texts tended to include more commas than is the case in modern texts. Commas were formerly inserted more widely in the belief that readers benefited from seeing which items within a sentence went together:

> *Parkinson noted that, according to the law of triviality,*
> *'The time spent on any item on the agenda will be in*
> *inverse proportion to the sum involved.'*

The modern tendency is to omit commas if the reader can understand the sentence clearly without them:

> *Parkinson noted that according to the law of triviality*
> *'The time spent on any item on the agenda will be in*
> *inverse proportion to the sum involved.'*

Colons

It was formerly considered acceptable to use a colon as an alternative to a semicolon when one part of a sentence balanced or contrasted with the other, as in:

> *To err is human: to forgive, divine.*

> *There were scowls and sneers from the two sisters: there were blushes and giggles from their friends.*

This usage is now regarded as old-fashioned, and a semicolon is considered to be the correct punctuation mark to use when linking balanced clauses:

> *To err is human; to forgive, divine.*

> *There were scowls and sneers from the two sisters; there were blushes and giggles from their friends.*

This allows colons to be reserved for the function of introducing a clarification or explanation.

Hyphens

The modern tendency is to use hyphens only when it is strictly necessary, with the result that written texts have much less hyphenation than used to be the case (see page 78).

Compound nouns are usually written as one word (*afterlife, catchphrase, dishcloth*) or two words (*blood vessel, castor oil, egg white*) when formerly they would have been written with a hyphen.

Moreover, many hyphens that served to avoid an awkward combination of letters are now often omitted, as people become more tolerant of unusual letter combinations (*battleaxe, earring, bookkeeping*).

MODERN PUNCTUATION TRENDS

Despite the modern tendency to dispense with hyphens, you should keep in mind that hyphens can be an extremely useful tool for making your writing easy to read, and they should not be left out when their absence would make the text ambiguous or unclear.

Dashes

The longer em dash (see pages 71–2) is used less commonly nowadays. It was formerly often used as a separating device, as in:

I don't mean to say he's incompetent—he certainly isn't.

In modern texts, a shorter en dash (see pages 71–2) is often used as a separator. Unlike the longer dash, the shorter dash is written with a space in front of and after it:

I don't mean to say he's incompetent – he certainly isn't.

The long em dash is also used less frequently as a substituting device in swearwords and expletives. These words are now often written instead with a series of asterisks or a combination of symbols:

He called the landlord a f***ing yokel.
He called the landlord a f*@!ing yokel.

Abbreviations

i
Abbreviations are discussed more fully on pages 125–30.

In keeping with the general trend in favour of more open punctuation, some punctuation marks that were once used to indicate abbreviations are now often omitted.

The traditional rule states that abbreviations that are created by omitting the final letters of a word should be followed by a full stop:

Prof. Khan will be visiting from Oct. 30 to Nov. 4.

However, it is now common to write many of these part-word abbreviations without a full stop:

Prof Khan will be visiting from Oct 30 to Nov 4.

It is also less common to see full stops used after abbreviations composed of a series of initial letters:

relations between the USA and countries of the former USSR

Some words that were once written with an apostrophe to indicate that they were abbreviations are now regarded as standard words and so are spelled without an apostrophe (see page 20). Nowadays it would be regarded as very old-fashioned to use an apostrophe when writing words such as *'plane* (for *aeroplane*) and *'flu* (for *influenza*), although you may still see an apostrophe used in older texts.

Addresses

Formerly, in both handwritten and typewritten letters, it was usual to follow each line of the address with a comma. A comma was also inserted after the house number, and a full stop came after any initials, as in:

Mr R. Galbraith,
5, Henderson Avenue,
ABERDEEN
AB3 6FG

MODERN PUNCTUATION TRENDS

Nowadays, in line with the general tendency to use the minimum amount of punctuation, these commas and full stops are usually omitted, particularly in typewritten letters or those produced on a computer:

Mr R Galbraith

5 Henderson Avenue

ABERDEEN

AB3 6FG

Checklist

1. **Commas**
   - modern style is to omit bracketing commas if the reader can understand the sentence clearly without them

2. **Colons**
   - in modern punctuation, they are not used as an alternative to a semicolon

3. **Hyphens**
   - modern style is to omit hyphens in compound nouns and write these as one or two words

4. **Dashes**
   - en dashes are now usually used in preference to em dashes as separators
   - a series of asterisks or a combination of symbols is now used to show an expletive

5. **Abbreviations**
   - full stops are now often omitted after abbreviations
   - apostrophes are omitted in front of short forms that are accepted as standard words

6. **Addresses**
   - commas and full stops are now often omitted from addresses

American punctuation style

So far, this book has dealt mainly with the rules and conventions of punctuation as practised in British English. However, American punctuation style differs from British style in several important aspects. British texts now tend to use minimal or 'open punctuation'. American texts, on the other hand, tend to be rather more conventional and strict in their approach. This chapter compares the two styles and summarizes the main differences between them.

Full stops in abbreviations

In American texts there is generally greater use of full stops in abbreviations than in modern British texts. Modern British style tends towards minimum punctuation and this includes the punctuation of most types of abbreviation. Thus, American texts prefer to keep full stops in abbreviations such as *e.g.* and *i.e.*, which are often written *eg* and *ie* in British texts.

i

Abbreviations are discussed more fully on pages 125–30.

Use of the serial comma

In lists of items, American texts often use a comma after the item in the list that is immediately followed by a conjunction (*and* or *or*). More often than not, the British omit this 'serial' comma. Compare the following examples:

> *Alice, Siobhan, and Liam will be coming to the party too.*
> [= American style]

Alice, Siobhan and Liam will be coming to the party too.
[= British style]

Are you going to have the fish, the salad, or the pasta?
[= American style]

Are you going to have the fish, the salad or the pasta?
[= British style]

Using a comma to link two clauses with the same subject

Where there is continuity of subject between the clauses of a sentence and the clauses are connected by a linking word or words, such as *and*, *because* and *in order*, British style regards the comma before the linking word as optional. American style prefers a comma before the linking word. Compare the following examples:

Malcolm is related to me by marriage, and is a regular houseguest.
[= American style]

Malcolm is related to me by marriage and is a regular houseguest.
[= British style]

Candida looked exhausted, because she had been travelling all night.
[= American style]

Candida looked exhausted because she had been travelling all night.
[= British style]

Commas in numbers

In American texts, numbers between 1000 and 9999 have a comma after the first number. The British tend not to use commas in four-figure numbers:

We estimate that the final figure will be between 1,300 and 2,500.
[= American style]

We estimate that the final figure will be between 1300 and 2500.
[= British style]

Quotation marks

In American texts, double quotation marks are used to enclose a quotation, whereas British style prefers single quotation marks. For a quotation within a quotation Americans use single quotes within double quotes, where the British would use double quotes within single quotes:

"At first she said, 'I don't think I should,' but then she said, 'Well, okay, just this once.'"
[= American style]

'At first she said, "I don't think I should", but then she said, "Well, okay, just this once".'
[= British style]

American texts have commas and full stops inside the closing quotation mark whether or not the punctuation 'belongs' to the quoted material. Compare the following examples:

Shakespeare describes England as 'this sceptred isle.'
[= American style]

Shakespeare describes England as 'this sceptred isle'.
[= British style]

Letters

In American texts a colon is used after the initial greeting in a letter (*Dear Sir:*) where in British English there would be a comma (*Dear Sir,*).

Checklist

1. **Full stops in abbreviations**
- American texts prefer to keep full stops in abbreviations

2. **Use of the serial comma**
- American texts prefer to use a serial comma

3. **Using a comma to link two main clauses with the same subject**
- American texts normally use a comma; British texts consider this optional

4. **Commas in numbers**
- American texts use commas in four-figure numbers such as *1,000*

5. **Quotation marks**
- American texts prefer double quotation marks as standard
- American texts always put punctuation marks inside the closing quotation mark

6. **Letters**
- American texts use a colon after the initial greeting

Part Three

Other Writing Conventions

Capital letters

Capital letters are not punctuation marks as such, but they perform a similar function in making writing easier to read, and so it is worth mentioning some points about their use in this book.

Full sentences and sentence fragments

As has been discussed in earlier chapters, ordinary sentences begin with a capital letter. This also applies to so-called sentence fragments. Here are some full sentences and sentence fragments with initial capitals:

> *She was running the hamburger stall, and I don't think she has ever worked so hard in her life. Poor girl.*
>
> *Will she ever find a decent job? Probably not for a while.*
>
> *You want me to give you five hundred dollars? No way!*

Proper names

A capital is used for the first letter of proper names: that is, for the names of people and places. Here are some examples:

> *Anne Ross*
>
> *Asia*
>
> *St Kitts and Nevis*
>
> *Kuala Lumpur*
>
> *Lake Winnipeg*
>
> *the Pacific Ocean*

CAPITAL LETTERS

Capitals are used for the titles of books, plays, films, newspapers, etc. When the title is made up of several words, it is usually only the most important words that are given capitals, unless an unimportant word such as *a* or *the* is the first word of the title. Here are some examples:

> *Three Men in a Boat*
>
> *The Merchant of Venice*
>
> *The Lion, the Witch and the Wardrobe*
>
> *The Sunday Times*
>
> *A Question of Sport*

In the same way, capitals are used for each important element in the official titles of people, institutions, organizations, buildings, etc. Here are some examples:

> *the Duke of Portland*
>
> *William the Conqueror*
>
> *the Foreign Secretary*
>
> *the Archbishop of Canterbury*
>
> *the Pope*
>
> *the House of Commons*
>
> *the Inland Revenue*

Note that when a title has been shortened but refers to a specific person or institution, the capital is retained, as in:

> *the Duke and his wife*
>
> *the Commons*
>
> *the Revenue*

However, when the title is used in a more general way and does not, therefore, refer to a specific individual, it is usually written without a capital, as in:

the dukes of Portland

the prime ministers of France and Spain

successive popes

He hopes to be a junior vice-president by the time he's thirty.

The names of days of the week, months and festivals start with a capital letter:

Friday the thirteenth

a sunny day in March

Easter Sunday

Hanukkah or the Festival of Lights

Note that the names of the seasons do not usually require a capital letter, but *Spring* may have a capital to distinguish it from the other senses of the word, as in:

He had a spring in his step, and Spring was in the air.

Words derived from proper names

In general, words that are derived from proper names also have an initial capital letter, as in:

Dickensian working conditions

Victorian architecture

Shakespearean tragedies

The names of languages and their related adjectives start with a capital:

He's studying French, Italian, Latin and Greek.

a Spanish phrasebook

We speak Urdu at home.

CAPITAL LETTERS

When a two-word phrase includes a proper name or an adjective denoting a country or region, that word is written with a capital letter if the association with the place remains strong:

>   *Brussels lace*
>   *French bread*
>   *Cornish pasty*
>   *Lancashire hotpot*

However, if the association with the place has been diminished by familiarity, these phrases are written without a capital:

>   *panama hat*
>   *italic type*
>   *guinea pig*

Brand names

In published writing, all brand names and trademarks mentioned should have a capital letter, even where the brand name has come to be used generically for a whole class of similar products, as is the case with *Hoover*®, *Sellotape*® and *Xerox*®. If a capital letter is not used, legal action may be taken by the manufacturer of the product.

In strict usage, brand names should not be used as verbs. However, it is in fact quite common to see brand names used as verbs, with no capital letter, as in:

>   *Have you hoovered the bedrooms yet?*
>   *I sellotaped a note to the door.*

Using capital letters for emphasis

Capital letters can sometimes be used as an alternative to italics or quotation marks when you want to highlight or emphasize a word or phrase. Capital letters are often used in this way in notices and advertisements:

> *Please do NOT smoke on the premises.*
>
> *This model has been reduced to HALF PRICE!*

i

This use of capital letters is especially useful when you do not have italics or bold available to you, as is often the case when writing e-mail and text messages. However, you should be aware that using capitals in e-mail is regarded by many people as the equivalent of shouting, and people are apt to think you are expressing anger or irritation if you use capitals freely in e-mail.

Abbreviations

For the use of capitals in abbreviations, see pages 125–30.

Checklist

1. **Full sentences and sentence fragments**
- sentences and sentence fragments begin with a capital letter

2. **Proper names**
- capitals are used for the first letter of the names of people and places
- capitals are used for the titles of books, plays, films, newspapers, etc
- capitals are used for each important element in the titles of people, institutions, organizations, buildings, etc
- capitals are used for days of the week, months and festivals

3. **Words derived from proper names**
- capitals are used for adjectives denoting a country or region
- capitals are used for languages and their related adjectives

4. **Brand names**
- should always have a capital letter
- sometimes used loosely as verbs without a capital letter

5. **Using capital letters for emphasis**
- as an alternative for italics or quotation marks, especially in notices or advertisements
- capital letters in e-mail are taken to express anger or annoyance

6. **Abbreviations**
- see pages 125–30

Abbreviations

Abbreviations are shortened forms of words or phrases. They are used principally to save space in writing, but they are also commonly used in speech when people want to avoid using a long or complicated title or name. An abbreviation often becomes so widely used that it is more familiar than the full form: the abbreviation *MP* is used as much as, and probably more than, the full form *member of parliament*; similarly, *BBC* is more familiar and readily understood by British people than *British Broadcasting Corporation*.

We can categorize abbreviations into four different types:

- Part-word abbreviations
- Contractions
- Initialisms
- Acronyms

Part-word abbreviations

A part-word abbreviation is a shortened form in which part of the word is written in place of the whole word. Traditionally, part-word abbreviations are followed by a full stop. Examples include:

> *Prof.* [= Professor]
>
> *Wed.* [= Wednesday]
>
> *Oct.* [= October]
>
> *approx.* [= approximately]
>
> *fem.* [= feminine]
>
> *derog.* [= derogatory]

ABBREVIATIONS

Abbreviations of this type should, in general, be avoided in formal writing, where it is customary to write out the full form:

> *Professor Khan will visit from Friday 28 October to Wednesday 2 November.*

Part-word abbreviations are, however, perfectly acceptable in less formal contexts, such as e-mail, and in certain specialized texts where space is at a premium:

> *Prof. Khan will visit from Fri. 28 Oct. to Wed. 2 Nov.*

As noted on page 111, it is becoming increasingly common to see part-word abbreviations written without a full stop, as long as this creates no confusion:

> *Prof Khan will visit from Fri 28 Oct to Wed 2 Nov.*

Abbreviated forms for units of measurement form a special class. These can be used in technical and scientific contexts where they are written without full stops:

> *This specimen is about 16cm long, but some are larger.*

In non-technical formal writing, words for measurements should be written out in full:

> *The poem was carved in letters ten centimetres high.*

Contractions

Contractions are shortened forms that include the **first and last letters** of the word being shortened. Abbreviations of this type are mostly used for conventional titles that come before names in letter writing, and in writing addresses. Examples include:

> *Mr* [= Mister]
>
> *Dr* [= Doctor]

St [= Saint]

Rd [= Road]

contd [= continued]

The following points should be noted:

- Contractions follow the form of the whole word. If the whole word starts with a capital letter, the contraction also starts with a capital letter.
- A full stop at the end of the contraction is optional. However, modern British usage generally prefers to omit the full stop unless its absence would lead to a misreading of the contraction.
- In e-mail and text messaging, contracted forms of familiar or frequently occurring words are common and, almost without exception, have no full stops.
- Contractions only appear in writing. They are unpronounceable as short forms and are read and pronounced as the full form would be, so that *Mr* is read and pronounced *Mister*, *St* is read and pronounced *Saint*, and so on.
- Some contractions are written with an apostrophe occurring where letters are omitted. These forms are discussed on pages 20–1.

Initialisms

Initialisms are abbreviations consisting of the first letter of each word in a group of words. They are distinct from acronyms (see below) in that each letter is **pronounced separately**.

In cases where the initials represent an organization or country, each initial is written as a capital letter, as in:

EU [= European Union]

UAE [= United Arab Emirates]

ABBREVIATIONS

In some abbreviated forms of organizations, the initial letter of a short word, such as *of*, is written as a lower-case letter, as in:

> *DfT* [= Department for Transport]
>
> *CoS* [= Chief of Staff]

When more than one letter from a word is taken into the abbreviation, the second and subsequent letters are usually in lower case, as in:

> *BEd* [= Bachelor of Education]
>
> *RAeS* [= Royal Aeronautic Society]

Many initialisms whose full forms are written in lower case are written with all their letters in lower case:

> *plc* [= public limited company]
>
> *aka* [= also known as]
>
> *asap* [= as soon as possible]

However, many of the new initialisms created for and used in e-mail and text messaging are written in capitals, even though they come from lower-case full forms:

> *BTW* [= by the way]
>
> *WRT* [= with regard to]
>
> *AFAIK* [= as far as I know]

In the past, most initialisms were written with full stops after each letter, but modern style prefers no full stops:

> *BBC* [= British Broadcasting Corporation]
>
> *CET* [= Central European Time]
>
> *GBH* [= grievous bodily harm]

The small number of initialisms that come from Latin phrases are written with lower-case letters and traditionally have full stops. Increasingly, however, these abbreviations too are written without full stops:

a.m. or *am* [= ante meridiem (before noon)]

p.m. or *pm* [= post meridiem (after noon)]

e.g. or *eg* [= exempli gratia (for example)]

i.e. or *ie* [= id est (that is)]

Usage

A word of warning about Latin abbreviations: they are often used inappropriately. For this reason, it is generally best to avoid them in formal writing and to rephrase the sentence or use an English equivalent.

Acronyms

Acronyms are abbreviations formed from the first letters of words to create a phrase which is **pronounced as a new word**. Acronyms are not followed by a full stop.

All the letters in the acronym may be written as capitals, and this is often the case for the titles of organizations or institutions, as in:

NATO [= North Atlantic Treaty Organization]

UNESCO [= United Nations Educational, Scientific and Cultural Organization]

Sometimes, acronyms may be written with only the first letter capitalized, as in:

Aids [= acquired immune deficiency syndrome]

Asean [= Association of South-East Asian Nations]

ABBREVIATIONS

A small number of acronyms have become so much more familiar than the full form of the phrase that they end up being treated like ordinary words and written entirely in lower-case letters, as in:

>   *radar* [= radio detecting and ranging]

>   *scuba* [= self-contained underwater breathing apparatus]

Punctuation after abbreviations that end in a full stop

When an abbreviation with a full stop after its last letter comes at the end of a sentence, there is no need to write another full stop:

✔ *He usually leaves for work around 7 a.m.*

✘ *He usually leaves for work around 7 a.m..*

✔ *We have moved from Jamaica St. to London Rd.*

✘ *We have moved from Jamaica St. to London Rd..*

However, when an abbreviation with a full stop after its last letter comes in the middle of a sentence, it may be followed by another punctuation mark:

>   *Tony usually leaves for work around 7 a.m., but today he was late.*

When an abbreviation with a full stop after its last letter comes at the end of a question or exclamation, the question mark or exclamation mark comes after the full stop:

>   *Did the train arrive at 8 p.m.?*

>   *You were supposed to be here at 6.30 p.m.!*

Checklist

1. Part-word abbreviations
- when part of the word is written for the full form
- traditionally followed by a full stop, but this is now often omitted
- should be avoided in formal writing
- abbreviations for units of measurement can be used in technical contexts and do not have a full stop

2. Contractions
- shortened forms that include the first and last letter of the word being shortened
- a full stop at the end of the contraction is optional and generally omitted
- read and pronounced as the full form would be

3. Initialisms
- when each initial letter is pronounced separately
- now usually written without full stops between the letters
- avoid initialisms that come from Latin phrases if you can

4. Acronyms
- when the first letters create a phrase that is pronounced as a new word
- not written with full stops

5. Punctuation after abbreviations that end in a full stop
- when an abbreviation with a full stop comes at the end of a sentence, there is no need to write another full stop
- when an abbreviation with a full stop comes in the middle of a sentence, it may be followed by another punctuation mark

Diacritics and accents

What is a diacritic?

A **diacritic** is any mark that appears above, below or sometimes through a letter and is used to indicate that the letter is to be pronounced in a particular way.

The marks that appear around letters to indicate pronunciation are often called *accents*, although this word should strictly be applied only to the marks over vowels. In written English, diacritics are usually only found in words that have been borrowed from other languages. You may well encounter the following diacritics:

acute accent	é
grave accent	è
circumflex accent	â
cedilla	ç
tilde	ñ
diaeresis or umlaut	ü
haček	š

An **accent** is a diacritic written or printed above a **vowel**, either to show that the vowel is to be pronounced in a certain way or to show that the vowel is stressed.

Writing words that contain diacritics

When you are writing a word that comes from a foreign language, you should try to include any diacritics. For handwritten work, this is easy enough to do. It is also possible to include the diacritics when you are using a computer, either by typing a special numerical code for a particular mark or selecting it from an on-screen display.

---
i

If you are using a computer, you can create the following diacritics (provided the 'Num Lock' feature is turned on) by holding down the 'Alt' key and typing the appropriate number:

à	0224
â	0226
ä	0228
ç	0231
è	0232
é	0233
ê	0234
ï	0239
ñ	0241
ô	0244
ö	0246
ü	0252

Many words borrowed directly from foreign languages have become so well established in English that they are no longer considered to be foreign words at all and are never spelt with an accent (eg *hotel*, from the French *hôtel*). Other borrowed words and phrases have not been fully assimilated into English and should be written with their diacritics. These include:

> *à la carte*
>
> *à la mode*
>
> *bête noire*
>
> *cause célèbre*
>
> *déjà vu*

mañana

raison d'être

señorita

tête-à-tête

Many French words are at an intermediary stage in the process of assimilation into English. For these, use of diacritics is now considered to be optional. Here are some common examples:

après-ski or *apres-ski*

café or *cafe*

clientèle or *clientele*

débris or *debris*

début or *debut*

divorcée or *divorcee*

fête or *fete*

naïve or *naive*

negligée or *negligee*

première or *premiere*

rôle or *role*

It is, however, better not to omit the diacritic in words where the accented letter would be pronounced differently (or not pronounced at all) in English. Words in this category include:

attaché

blasé

cliché

communiqué

façade

fiancé

passé

risqué

soufflé

soupçon

Checklist

1. **What is a diacritic?**
- *diacritic* refers to a mark written over, below or through any letter
- *accent* refers specifically to a mark over a vowel to show pronunciation or stress

2. **Writing words that contain diacritics**
- words that are regarded as standard English words do not require diacritics
- words that are not yet regarded as standard English words require diacritics
- diacritics are optional for words that are at an intermediate stage of acceptance
- use the diacritic if it helps to show how a word is pronounced

Numbers, fractions and dates

This chapter deals with writing numbers, fractions and dates in non-technical texts. In technical writing, it is customary to use numerals to represent numbers, rather than writing them out in words.

Writing numbers and fractions

Words or numerals?

In formal texts, small numbers should be written out in words as *one*, *two*, *three*, and so on:

✔ *a house with four bedrooms*

✘ *a house with 4 bedrooms*

✔ *I couldn't possibly eat three of them.*

✘ *I couldn't possibly eat 3 of them.*

It is quite acceptable to write larger numbers using numerals, especially where the full written form would produce a cumbersome appearance:

> *France produces 246 different types of cheese.*
>
> *The majority of the population is made up of people between the ages of 45 and 89.*
>
> *The rally was attended by 750 people.*

---

i

There is no fixed number above which you should start writing numbers as numerals. Some people prefer to write out all numbers from one to ninety-nine as words. However, in modern texts it is quite common to see all the numbers above twelve written as numerals. The important thing is that you should be consistent about the point at which you start using numerals.

There are a couple of occasions when it does not matter whether the number is large or small. If a sentence starts with a number, the number should always be written out in words:

✔ *Seven hundred and fifty people turned up for the rally.*

✘ *750 people turned up for the rally.*

Fractions should also be written out in words:

✔ *Cindy kept at it all morning, but only finished a quarter of the work.*

✘ *Cindy kept at it all morning, but only finished ¼ of the work.*

When a sentence contains an address, the street or building number is written in numerals, as it would be on a letter or envelope, whether or not it is a small or large number:

> *You might want to visit the National Postal Museum at 2 Massachusetts Avenue, Washington DC.*

Hyphens in numbers

Fractions that are made up of two parts are written with a hyphen:

> *Nearly three-quarters of these children are seriously undernourished.*

> *A kilometre is about five-eighths of a mile.*

Two-part numbers in the range from twenty-one to ninety-nine are also written with a hyphen:

> *There are twenty-four letters in the Greek alphabet.*

> *The majority of the population is made up of people between the ages of forty-five and eighty-nine.*

Note, however, there is no hyphen if you have to write a number of hundreds, thousands, etc:

> *Seven hundred and fifty people turned up for the rally.*

> *Three hundred and twenty-three people applied for the job.*

> *Twenty-six thousand fans filled the stadium.*

Commas in numbers

Numbers with five or more digits are written either with thin spaces or commas before every three digits counting from the right, like this:

> *14 575 or 14,575*

> *2 753 000 or 2,753,000*

Four-figure numbers are usually written with no spaces between the digits, and no comma, as in:

> *The match was watched by a crowd of 7043.*

Writing dates

Order of day, month and year

The usual way of writing dates in formal and business writing is in the following order:

> *day number + name of the month + year*

It is not necessary to add commas between the elements:

> *The Battle of Culloden took place on 16 April 1746.*

However, it is also acceptable to write dates with a comma after the month, or with the letters *th*, etc after the day number:

> *The Battle of Culloden took place on 16 April, 1746.*
> *The Battle of Culloden took place on 16th April 1746.*
> *The Battle of Culloden took place on 16th April, 1746.*

It is also possible to write dates using numerals for all the elements, as in *12/7/05*. However, it is best to be aware that this way of writing the date is understood differently in Britain and America, and so can cause confusion. In America 12/7/05 means '7 December 2005', while in Britain it means '12 July 2005'.

For more information on the use of the comma in dates, see page 39.

Ranges of dates

For periods of time that are expressed in terms of a starting date and closing date, the two dates can be linked either by an en dash (see pages 71–2) or by the words *to* or *and*. Remember that it is incorrect to use the dash if you have already started to indicate the range by writing *between* or *from*:

✔ *30 August 1918–5 July 2002*

✔ *1918–2002*

✗ *from 15–25 June 2005*

✔ *from 15th to 25th June 2005*

✗ *between 1999–2005*

✔ *between 1999 and 2005*

NUMBERS, FRACTIONS AND DATES

When you use a dash to link years or other periods of time in this way, it is common practice to use as few digits as possible, and so you need not repeat digits in the second date:

> 1902–8
>
> 1923–36

However, when the range includes two different centuries, all the figures must be written, as in:

> 1837–1901
>
> 1999–2005

AD and BC

Sometimes, a year is written with the abbreviation _AD_ (*anno domini*) or _BC_ (*before Christ*). In printed texts, these abbreviations are usually in small capitals, rather than ordinary capitals. _AD_ is usually written before the year, as in _AD 1003_. _BC_ is written after the year, as in _274 BC_. To avoid misinterpretation, it is important to remember that pairs of years with the abbreviation _BC_ should include all the figures for both years, as in _251–224 BC_. If this range was written as _251–24 BC_, it would be indistinguishable from _251 BC–24 BC_.

Checklist

1. Writing numbers and fractions

- write small numbers in words and larger numbers in numerals
- two-part numbers from twenty-one to ninety-nine are written with a hyphen
- numbers with five or more digits are written either with thin spaces or commas before every three digits

2. Writing dates

- the usual order is: day number + name of the month + year
- two dates can be linked either by an en dash or by words, but not a combination of the two
- for ranges of years, use as few digits as possible, but when the range includes two different centuries, all the figures must be written
- *AD* is usually written before the year; *BC* is written after the year

Typefaces, fonts and layout

If you are using a computer, you can use different styles of type and page design to make your writing easier and more interesting to read. This can sometimes do the work that is traditionally done by punctuation.

Italics

Italics are letters that slope to the right, like this: *italic letters*. In printed texts, italics are used in the following ways:

Titles and names

As mentioned earlier, italics can be used for the titles of major works, such as books, plays, films, newspapers and works of art (see pages 55–6). Minor titles, such as magazine articles, songs and poems within a larger collection, are usually shown by quotation marks rather than italics:

> My brother is a huge fan of *The Lord of the Rings*.

> We studied *Macbeth* and *A Man for All Seasons* for GCSE English.

> *Highway 61 Revisited* contains such classic songs as 'Like a Rolling Stone' and 'Desolation Row'.

The names used in legal cases are usually written in italics:

> *Chapman* v *Penderley*

(Note that the 'v' is not printed in italic.)

The names of ships, aircraft and spacecraft are also italicized, as in:

> The battleships *Musashi* and *Yumato* were both sunk in World War II.

> Lindbergh's plane was called *Spirit of St Louis.*

> the voyages of the *Starship Enterprise*

Emphasis

Italics can be used to draw attention to a word or words that the writer wants to emphasize, as in:

> I *quite* agree.

> Why don't you make *him* do the washing up for a change.

Talking about words

You can also use italics instead of quotation marks when you are talking about words:

> The fool had written *unspeakable* instead of *unshakable.*

Foreign words and phrases

Foreign words and phrases that are not fully accepted as part of standard English are often printed in italics:

> Smoking was her particular *bête noire.*

> Eduardo grew up amid the *favelas* of Rio de Janeiro.

Once a foreign word has become very familiar in English, it usually loses its italics, although italics may be kept as a convenient way of distinguishing the word from a similarly spelt English word:

> a bottle of *sake*

Genus and species names

Biological genus and species names are conventionally printed in italic type, as in:

> *Digitalis purpurea* is the scientific name for the foxglove.

> The jaguar (*Panthera onca*) inhabits woodland and savannah close to water.

Note, however, that higher levels of classification, such as families and kingdoms, are not italicized:

> Dormice belong to the Gliridae family of rodents.

If you are not using a computer, you can <u>underline</u> words that you want to show as being italicized.

Bold letters

Bold letters are letters that are printed in a heavier, darker way than normal, so as to stand out from the surrounding text, like this: **bold letters**. In printed texts, bold letters are used in the following ways:

Chapter and section titles

Because bold letters attract attention more strongly than other letters, they are used for the titles of chapters and sections.

Emphasis

Bold letters can also be used as an alternative to italics when you want to highlight or emphasize a word or phrase:

> As a general rule, **never** add an apostrophe to form a plural.

> Remember that these tablets should be taken **no more than three times a day**.

This use of bold letters is especially useful when you have already used italics for a different feature of the text.

Page layout

Besides allowing you to create bold and italic letters, a computer also allows you to change various features of the page to create a look that is both attractive and in keeping with the message you are trying to communicate. Paying attention to the following aspects of page layout can enhance your writing considerably:

Fonts

i
A font is a particular style of letters or characters used in printed text.

Using a computer gives you access to a wide array of different fonts. Changing the font can give a document a very different look and create a very different impression on your readers.

The font you decide to use will probably depend on the impression you wish to create:

> Using a formal font, such as Courier, will help you to create a serious tone for reports.

> Using an informal font, such as Comic Sans, will give your writing a relaxed tone for personal letters and e-mails.

> *Using a highly decorative font, such as Monotype Corsiva, may enhance a flyer or an invitation.*

Type size

You can vary the size of type you use for a document so that the text fits neatly onto the page and does not leave a lot of empty space.

In a longer document, you can use different sizes of type for different parts of the document. For example, you may decide to use a larger size of type for headings, or a smaller size of type for footnotes.

Margins

Using wider margins creates a narrower column of text and means that fewer words can fit onto each line. Changing the width of the margins can therefore be another way of ensuring the text fits neatly into the required space.

Computers also allow you to decide whether to 'justify' the text (so that the margins are straight, as in this book) or leave a 'ragged' margin. Having straight margins tends to give a more formal, authoritative look to a document, whereas a ragged right-hand margin can make it appear more informal and accessible.

Spacing

Using double-spaced text is another way of spreading out the text to fit the required space. Double-spaced text also gives more room for readers to write comments in, and so may be required for essays or reports.

Visual features

A written document can make use of various features to draw attention to particular words, paragraphs and types of information. For example, you can use different colours for special types of information, or you can surround important text with a border to draw your readers' attention to it.

You can also insert pictures and diagrams into a piece of writing to make it more visually interesting. Moreover, some points are easier to explain or illustrate by visual images than by words alone, and so a thoughtfully placed illustration can often be more effective than a lengthy explanation.

Other features that you might think of using include tables, which can serve to set out information so it can be easily interpreted, and bullet points, which present lists in an eye-catching manner.

If used successfully, all of these features can make it easier for your readers to grasp what you are trying to say. Like conventional punctuation marks, they do the job of showing how the text might be read aloud, what information goes together and what is especially important.

Checklist

1. **Italics**
   - used for titles, names in legal cases, names of ships, planes, etc
   - used instead of quotation marks for emphasis or when talking about words
   - used for foreign words and phrases
   - used for genus and species names

2. **Bold letters**
   - used for chapter and section titles
   - used for emphasis

3. **Page layout**
   - think about the most appropriate font, type size, margins and spacing
   - use features such as colour and bullet points to highlight important information and present facts as clearly as possible

Solutions

Solutions

The full stop

A   1   *Tom was planning a surprise party for Jerry.*

    2   *Cindy stayed at home and tried on her new shoes.*

    3   *Add the butter and the condensed milk.*

    4   *My e-mail address, jane@eazynet.co.uk, is easy to remember.*

B   Beside herself with rage and humiliation, she paced the floor grinding her teeth. She was so focussed on thoughts of revenge that she didn't hear the door opening. It wasn't until her mother was standing in her line of vision that she became aware that someone was actually witnessing her inarticulate mutterings and oaths. She stopped in her tracks, suddenly more embarrassed than angry.

The question mark

A   1   *Did I ask you about your trip to Italy?*

    2   *Whether she will come now is anybody's guess.*

    3   *The question that immediately comes to mind on reading the report is why this problem was not identified earlier.*

    4   *I don't suppose you would give some thought as to how we can improve the situation?*

B   Was it only four hours since her sisters had gone to the party? She asked herself whether they would come

back soon and tell her all about it. In the meantime
there was not much point sitting around and dreaming. The housework would not do itself, would it?
Cindy looked around for the duster. Where on earth
had she left it?

The exclamation mark

A　1　*What a glorious sunset!*

　　2　*Stop making that horrible noise immediately.*
　　　[An exclamation mark would also be possible]

　　3　*The committee is extremely enthusiastic about your*
　　　proposal.

　　4　*Wasn't that a fantastic save by the goalkeeper!*

B　　'I don't believe it! We leave you alone for one day and
　　you turn the house into a disaster area! There isn't a
　　scrap of food anywhere. What on earth have you been
　　doing?' Her stepmother stormed off into the other
　　room. Five seconds later she screamed out, 'Good grief!
　　Somebody is asleep in my bed!'

The apostrophe

A　1　*It's time we put the budgie back in its cage.*

　　2　*They'll get back home at about one o'clock in the*
　　　morning our time.

　　3　*I couldn't brake quickly enough and now my son's*
　　　bike has a buckled front wheel.

　　4　*It's all curled up into a ball so you can't see it's head.*

　　5　*Isn't this anyone's newspaper? If it isn't, I'll take it*
　　　home with me.

　　6　*I've been reading Keats' poems.*

　　7　*You'll have to decide which is yours and which is hers.*

　　8　*One's financial situation is surely one's own business?*

B	1	*the house of my father*	*my father's house*
	2	*the workshop of the blacksmith*	*the blacksmith's workshop*
	3	*the children of the Smiths*	*the Smiths' children*
	4	*the toys of the children*	*the children's toys*
	5	*the masts of the boats*	*the boats' masts*
	6	*the surgery of Dr Charles*	*Dr Charles's [or Charles'] surgery*
	7	*the rear wheel of the Mercedes*	*the Mercedes' rear wheel*

The comma

A   1   *It was the longest, most boring journey I've ever had to endure.*

2   *He had a big lump on his head, a fractured wrist, a bruise on his cheek, and a small cut above his right eye.*

3   *The driver braked violently and, flinging open the car door, jumped out and grabbed the boy by the collar.*

4   *Even in 1950, however, beer production was largely regional, if not local, and there were still some 310 firms with 540 separate breweries.*

5   *As the train pulled into the station, heads popped out of every window.*

6   *Hey, Harry, have you got a moment?*

7   *Clumsily, like a fallen horse righting itself, she scrambled to her feet, gathered up the bananas, marshmallows, umbrella, thermos, handbag, and other possessions that had fallen or rolled around her, and, waving reassuringly, walked briskly away.*

B   Tom, who had been standing around idly in the street, saw his friend approaching. Jerry was carrying a large bag, which was stuffed full of eggs, cheese, tomatoes and mushrooms. 'Hey, Jerry, where have you been?' 'I was feeling hungry, so I decided to go to the shops and get some food so I could make a big, tasty omelette.'

The colon

1   *Here is the fruit you asked me to get: a pound of grapes, four oranges and half a dozen bananas.*

2   *The Life of Oscar Wilde: Tragedy or Farce?*

3   *I'm sure I've packed everything: suntan lotion, swimwear, mosquito repellent, film for the camera, passports and money.*

4   *This is exactly what I wanted: a room with a view over the harbour.*

The semicolon

1   *Dickens is my favourite author; Trollope is a close second.*

2   *You shouldn't regard this as a setback; see it instead as a pause for reflection.*

3   *The country's wealth was built on the more traditional industries of steel-making, shipbuilding and heavy engineering; textiles, clothing and carpet manufacture; pottery and glassmaking; and coal-mining.*

4   *Both France and Italy have had to take steps to reduce government spending; consequently, the unemployment rate in both countries has risen significantly.*

Quotation marks

1   *It was in this film that the character played by Michael Douglas famously said, 'Lunch is for wimps.'*

2 *'Are we there yet?' asked Bart.*

3 *'I am pretty sure,' said Pete, 'that it will be ready before Saturday.'*

4 *I don't use the words 'absolute genius' lightly.*

5 *"Next week we'll examine the 'stream of conscious-ness' technique in greater detail," the tutor announced.*

6 *They spoke a very archaic form of English full of 'thou's and 'thee's.*

Brackets

1 *His wife (odd as it may seem) is a keep-fit instructor.*

2 *The house sparrow (Passer domesticus) has grey and brown plumage.*

3 *The use of bleaches is explained in Chapter 10 (pages 56–62).*

4 *Her collection includes records from the 1960s (for example Marvin Gaye, The Shadows and Dusty Springfield) as well as more recent music.*

5 *Jerry has a passion for Italian cheeses (eg Pecorino and Mozzarella), but also enjoys some British cheeses (eg Double Gloucester and Red Leicester).*

The dash

1 *A majority of those polled on Tuesday and Wednesday (55% and 57% respectively) do not believe the president should resign.*

2 *Josh or Nick (I'm not sure which) will pick you up from the station tomorrow.*

3 *In his attempt to secure the succession for his strongly Protestant daughter-in-law, Warwick – now duke of Northumberland – failed dismally.*

The slash

1   *This car can't manage much more than 80 km/h.*
2   *They talked about recording an old Lennon/McCartney song.*
3   *Your ticket will expire at the end of the 2010/2011 season.*
4   *Didn't I see you on the London/York train?*
5   *Please bring your passport/proof of identity with you.*

The hyphen

1   *Harry is a top-class performer on the cello.*
2   *She was sitting on a bench eating a fried-egg sandwich.*
3   *Jane was selected to ice-skate in the Olympics.*
4   *Heffernan chipped in with three second-half goals.*
5   *This book has been printed on acid-free paper.*

Which punctuation mark?

1   *Luis asked me if I had ever visited South America.*
2   *Can you all give your names to the officer.*
3   *I am a keen tennis player, but my husband prefers to play golf.*
4   *Jared is Capricorn; Dylan is a Libra.*
5   *Sonya remembered why she hated this place: it was too cold.*
6   *My brother is – it pains me to say – more successful than I am.*
7   *Strawberries are, in my opinion, much nicer than raspberries.*

Punctuating speech and quotations

1   *'Do you actually like oysters?' Bob enquired.*

2   *Was it Peter or Harry who asked, 'Will we be paid expenses?'*

3   *'Stop making that horrible noise immediately!' she bellowed.*

4   *John suddenly shouted, 'Look out! He's got a gun!'*

5   *'I was', said Frank, 'completely terrified.'*

6   *'If you understand the problem,' said Amy, 'the answer is obvious.'*

Index

INDEX